A

BESTIARY

A

BESTIARY

LILY

HOANG

A Bestiary
FIRST EDITION

Copyright © 2016 Lily Hoang
all rights reserved
Printed in the United States of America

ISBN
978·0·9963167·4·3
DESIGN ≈ SEVY PEREZ
text in Brandon Grotesque and Adobe Caslon Pro

ooooo

This book is published by the

Cleveland State University Poetry Center
csupoetrycenter.com
2121 Euclid Avenue, Cleveland, Ohio 44115-2214

and is distributed by

SPD / Small Press Distribution, Inc.
spdbooks.org
1341 Seventh Street Berkeley, California 94710-1409

ooooo

A CATALOG RECORD FOR THIS TITLE IS
AVAILABLE FROM THE LIBRARY OF CONGRESS

CONTENTS

THIS BOOK IS FOR CARMEN,
FOREVER MY SISTER IN WORDS AND IN LIFE.

INTRODUCTION

Once upon a time—shh, shh—this is only a fairy tale.

on the RAT RACE

It is not a desire to play games: it is an urge, a yearning, an addiction.

∞∞∞

When I was young, my sister went to prison. I don't know why she went because no one will tell me.

My sister died nearly three years ago.

I stopped asking why before once upon a time began.

I have re-named her my dead sister.

Although born in the year of the monkey, my dead sister was a real rat. I admire that about her. Sometimes I can be a rodent, too.

∞∞∞

My mother and I play games on our electronic devices. It's early, maybe five in the morning, the sun has not yet lifted darkness from the sky, and we're both up and tapping away at our iPads. My mother had stayed up late playing too. I fell asleep after midnight, and she was playing. I woke up to get a sip of water, and she was playing. I got up to go to the bathroom, and she was playing. I woke up, too early, and she was still playing. I wondered then—as now—if she'd slept at all or if the games she played induced a certain desired insomnia, one pressured by compulsion and pleasure. Or maybe she had been excited that I was home visiting and that had kept her awake. Or maybe this was her natural circadian. Or maybe there was something else bothering her, an icy ache.

∞∞∞

My dead sister left behind two sons: one has become healthy, the other a heroin addict—a *recovering* heroin addict.

∞∞∞

B.F. Skinner created the operant conditioning chamber. Rats were taught that pushing a lever would release food. Then, a variety of stimulants were applied, such as electroshock. The purpose of the operant conditioning chamber was to study schedules of reinforcement, discriminative control, delayed response, and punishment.

ooooo

Towards the end, my dead sister stopped discriminating: any opiate would do, anything to subside her pain.

ooooo

My ex-husband Chris used to tell me I compartmentalize my problems in order to focus on work. This was a criticism, but to me, my abilities to neatly tuck my problems into a liminal space and heave myself into writing and teaching is an admirable trait, one that other people praise. To push one of those compartments away from the shadows and into the uproarious sunlight is to assail me. To point out my difference feels like a massacre of my dignity and my very personhood. The aggressor doesn't recognize my hurt because I work my best not to show it.

ooooo

Rats have been used in laboratories since the early 20th century.

ooooo

When I was a girl, my parents' Vietnamese friends would say, "Your sister is so beautiful, but at least you are smart."

At her funeral, the Vietnamese community gathers and praises her beauty.

My dead sister was buried in my wedding *áo dài.* Now that I am no longer married, I don't need any trinkets.

ooooo

A rat race is a pursuit without end. It is a lab rat rolling in its wheel, sniffing hard for the prize that can only be had when the goal is reached—but the rat is never freed and the race is only over until tomorrow.

At the end of the rat race is a Styrofoam carrot, but doesn't it look delicious?

ooooo

David Foster Wallace said, "The alternative is unconsciousness, the default setting, the rat race, the constant gnawing sense of having had, and lost, some infinite thing."

ooooo

Once, many years ago, my dead sister achieved the American dream—and then she lost it, destroyed it, abandoned it—as she had with me, too.

But before all that, she met a military man, whom she married. She sold her multi-million dollar construction company, and they lived in a tour of Midwestern two-stories houses. He was a Full Bird Colonel in the Air Force and she felt very alone.

ooooo

A group of congregated rats is called a mischief.

ooooo

One Thanksgiving many years ago, my dead sister flew my whole family to Colorado Springs. Mason was just a baby then and Justin an angry teen and my parents were proud. She showed my parents her husband's paycheck as proof of her happiness. She smiled and I recognized her misery.

She was still fat with baby weight even though Mason was nearly a year old. For Christmas, her husband gave her diet pills—as a joke, supposedly.

He was a good man though. He didn't deserve any of it.

∞∞∞

The Rat King is not king of rats.
  The Rat King is a monster.
  He is the plague. And gross.

∞∞∞

Then, a decade into their marriage, everything busted open—first her lies and addiction, then Mason's paternity was revealed, and finally the fact that she had drained all of their accounts and savings and stocks. She went to rehab to keep her sons, and her husband attempted to forgive her.
  She moved back to San Antonio, a failure.
  She got a brain aneurysm.
  By forty, she had moved back in my parents.
  By forty-three, she was dead.

∞∞∞

In those years between losing her American dream life and dying, she seemed genuinely happy. Her long-time lover and Mason's real father loved her immensely, worshipped her. Raul devoted himself to her, and she's always preferred to be spoiled. Her death is tragic because happiness is rare. I was witness to it.

∞∞∞

When my father is up and drinking his coffee, I show him a logic game I think he'd like, 2048. My mother asks me to download it onto her iPad too. Insensitively, I say, "It's a hard game."
  My mother says, "I think the games I play are too kid-like."
  The games my mother plays are, in fact, made for children. These

are the games she feels most attuned to and prepared for. They approximate what she approximates her own competence to be. Despite her invisible self-confidence, my mother is now a translator for the courts. She travels all over Texas. She is a valued commodity. Her job, albeit part-time, betrays my mother's gentle and cunning intelligence.

I download different games for my mother. This time, I don't rely on Disney princesses or animated animals. I get her a mega-solitaire pack. I find her more challenging games, ones that might retain her interest without being too difficult as to usher in defeat. I curate a gallery of participatory entertainment.

Afterwards, I show my mother how to cut and paste on her iPad. She shakes her head and says, in English, "Ayyyyi, your mom so stupid."

In Vietnamese, I respond, "No, you're not stupid. You just didn't know, that's all."

"Listen to her," my father says.

∞∞∞

In the 1950s, Mao Zedong began the Four Pests campaign to rid China of rats, mosquitos, flies, and sparrows. The sparrows were a particular nuisance and the spotlight of his campaign. Nearly 80,000 scarecrows were built and erected. By decree, citizens were to force sparrows to fly until death by exhaustion. Knocking pots against pans, sparrows fell, and hundreds of millions of sparrows are estimated to have died this way.

But sparrows are useful, as are rats and mosquitos and flies. A nuisance, yes, but functional. And so the Chinese government learned about ecosystems: sparrows eat insects who eat grains and thus began the Great Famine.

∞∞∞

My father says to me in Vietnamese, "Your mother is never home. Now that she's retired, every day she has to go to the store and she has to go do this and she has to go do that." In English, he adds,

"She never stay with me." He pouts.

I have watched his desires turn adolescent, child-like: he wants shiny pretty things, and my mother. He still wants my mother.

∞∞∞

As a military housewife, my dead sister would hide away in her garage and smoke cigarettes and talk to her lover on the phone. She promised him she was getting a divorce, that he was the only man for her, that her husband was abusive and she was scared. Not knowing any better and deeply in love, Raul said, "I'll kill him." The success of the true rat race is all veneer. It is a hot-boxed garage and infidelity.

∞∞∞

The night before the night I find my dead sister seizing on her bedroom floor, before she went and died, I heard her crawling along the carpet. I heard her open my bags. I heard snaps and zippers. I didn't open my eyes.

∞∞∞

In Art Speigelman's *Maus*, the Nazis are cats and the Jews are mice. In Roberto Bolaño's "Police Rat," it is the rat who guards and protects, but only his own.

∞∞∞

Before I departed for my very first day of pre-K, my father disturbed his morning ritual of news and coffee to talk to me. It was an occasion. "We are yellow people," he said. He lifted his hands towards me, pushing his palms towards the ground. "Yellow skin."

I looked at my skin and his. Our skin wasn't yellow. But it wasn't my skin they laughed at anyway. It was my eyes, their slant, which I couldn't even identify as different.

"Yellow skin mean not as good. Do you understand?"

Although I didn't understand, I shook my head to indicate that I had.

"Yellow skin mean you have to work twice as hard as white people. Or they never respect you."

My father's broken English resonated with my own experience in school, and so I worked harder and felt proud when I was recognized as different. In elementary school, I was proud to be Vietnamese. I had not learned self-shame. And I have not attained that same level of confidence since. My naïveté was a power that experience has drained.

∞∞∞∞

A rat king is a group of rats melded together by the tail, whether through blood or encrusted trash. They grow together, so entangled, and when you see a rat king: run!

∞∞∞∞

My insomnia wakes me early—2am, some days, no later than 5am, ever, no matter what time I fall asleep—with a panic attack that I'm behind. It's early and I'm already behind. Sleeping on the couch in my parents' house aggravates this insomnia: I barely sleep at all.

It is in these quiet hours, these witching hours, that my mother and I are closest. We usually don't talk because my father is sleeping right next to us, but we are connected by our alertness at a time that betrays our anxiety and strife.

My parents' couches are a nice polished leather, but their dogs have frayed all the edges. Here is their nice house and their nice things: evidence of their hard work, their immigrant success: wearing thin, cheap, an imitation that shatters.

My mother disrupts our quiet with a groan of pain. I know my mother's sounds. There are the *tsk*'s that signal disappointment. There are the *aiiiiya*'s that show more disappointment. There is the sorrow of mourning, the sound my mother made as her daughter was buried, first, and then her sister, a year later. And there is pain, physical pain. The pain of cancer and chemo. The pain of growing old. The pain of disappointment forced onto her body.

"Look at my finger," my mother says.

It's crooked.

"Sometimes it just cramps like that. Look," my mother says, "I can't even hold a pen to write anymore." She shows me the only way she can hold a pen. It's awkward and unnatural. She has coped with this pain like it's supposed to be this way.

I hold in my urine. It's only recently that I realized this about myself. I hold it in for hours after recognizing the need for relief. I live in a perpetual state of pain and call it my own.

"Vietnamese women suffer better than all other people," my mother used to tell me. This morning, she repeats it again, "Vietnamese women suffer better than all other people."

I say, "You should go to the doctor. This isn't right."

"Yes," she says, "that's right." Her voice contains epiphany, like she hasn't thought of it before. "I should go to the doctor."

I look over to the counter. My parents' medications are stacked in rows and columns. They keep it all in the kitchen for convenience.

Games are her escape, and she can barely play because her hands aren't working any more.

ooooo

In Alaska, in order to rid the island of rodents, the government doused the land and air with poison. The island is called Rat Island. Rat Island has been free of rats since 2010.

A reporter says he was interested in the story because it offers "success" and "hope."

ooooo

To prove our renowned endurance of pain, Vietnamese women adorn their wrists with jade bracelets. In order to get the damn thing on, one must distort the hand, almost breaking it. I have yellow bruises for days, and yet: this is proof of our delicacy: how well we take that agony and internalize it. The tighter the fit, the more suffering the woman can persevere, the more beautiful she is considered.

ooooo

A knockout rat is a genetically engineered rat with a single gene turned off through a targeted mutation.

∞∞∞∞

When I visit, my mother always takes me to buy bras. It's our thing. My mother has been translating a lot and she is sad, so today, she is extravagant in her purchases. She picks up shirt after shirt and asks what I think.

"It's a little young for me. And small." I know she isn't suggesting it's for me. I am being a spoiled brat. I am being petty.

She picks up a blouse with the shoulder's cut out. "That's too sexy, that's what Dad would say." The only word I say in English is *sexy* because I don't know the Vietnamese translation, but also because I want to make a point.

She buys it anyway.

In the car, she says she will wear a blazer over all those blouses. "They are just for the inside," she says. "Besides," she says, "I don't like to wear anything that shows my arms because they're so ugly."

∞∞∞∞

Games are not necessarily about victory. The process of learning requires failure.

∞∞∞∞

Rats, in their little boxed mazes.

My sister, in her military boxed garage. Hidden away.

∞∞∞∞

A king who does not rule.

∞∞∞∞

My brother is paid to be a pacer, but he'd do it for free. He is addicted. He runs a 5-6 minute mile for twenty-six point two of them.

It started in high school, because his girlfriend called him "fat boy."

It started in elementary school, because my mother refused to give him a second bowl of *phở*.

Now he is so thin that he may weigh less than me, but his body is compressed muscles laid taut against bone.

∞∞∞

To account for immigration, my dead sister used to tell people she was a princess in Vietnam.

∞∞∞

My parents arrived in America and landed in Pennsylvania. It's cold there, an opposite climate to Vietnam: snow, ice, coats they did not yet have, could not yet afford.

Once, when my brother was six and my sister was seven and my parents were at work at a factory, my mother paid a neighbor lady to watch the kids after school. She forgot. My sister huddled close to the apartment, where heat might escape through the tiny gap between the door and the floorboards. My brother wet his pants because he could not find a bathroom and did not know enough English to ask.

∞∞∞

I work in public in order to not play games, something about surveillance and shame. With so many witnesses, games are for children, not adults with real jobs.

I admit my immaturity. If asked, I would say games activate different parts of the brain, but I don't know if that's true: say it with enough confidence and it will be. If asked, I would say games give me time to reflect and understand that which I do not yet know.

∞∞∞

As refugees, my parents wanted for their children American success with Vietnamese values.

In high school, if my father caught a teenager talking back to her parents on American television, he would say, "White kids no respect their parents."

"Dad," I would say in Vietnamese, "it's just TV." But he was right.

ooooo

The first time I met my ex-husband Chris's parents, they took us to Chinese food and his dad asked him about the LSAT. After dinner, he said, "Did you hear how they humiliated me?"

I asked, "Because they talked all slow and loud to me like I don't understand English?"

He said, "What?" and hurricaned his way inside to scream at them for trying to rule his life. I went outside to smoke a cigarette. I should've broken up with him then for disrespecting his parents. That should've been the first warning sign of our unavoidable failure, his irreconcilable temper, my default to victimhood, but I was blind with a love that ruined me.

ooooo

But I was not ruined forever: I refuse to give him that victory.

ooooo

Jade bracelets cannot be taken off. They break with indelicacy.

ooooo

I am safe because I belong to the most successful minority group. Our men are emasculated and our women praise their endurance of pain. We are a safe bunch, just shooting for assimilation and acceptance.

I hate this about myself as much as I am proud of my success.

ooooo

To pass time, I used to draw elaborate mazes. I never tried to solve them, I just liked to build.

ooooo

When I was young, my sister used to steal money from my parents, from their friends, from anyone really.

Once, she broke into our father's bathroom, where he kept his gun and all his money. She shattered a window from the inside and threw his gun into the front yard and stole all his savings. Our windows had black steel burglar bars, that's how we knew no one came in from the outside.

ooooo

When my dead sister's dream life began its descent, she ate a bottle of her husband's father's Percocet. They found her crawling under the Christmas tree, her hands full of pre-paid credit cards and cash. The envelopes made rainbow confetti.

She said, "I'll kill myself."

And her husband the military man did not take a suicide threat lightly, it's in his training. He called me from the psychiatric ward, and I could either tell him the truth or lie for my sister. Except that I didn't know which was which any more.

ooooo

The Morris water navigation task was developed by Richard Morris in 1981. Unlike typical rat mazes, the Morris water maze is open, without corridor. A large pool is filled with water. The temperature is carefully monitored so as to not shock the rat upon entrance. A small platform protrudes about an inch from the water's surface. This is the goal. There is no food at the end, no extra-sensory stimulus.

Although rats can swim, they don't like it.

Rats, when initially submerged, stay close to the pool's edge. The rat must be guided to the free-floating platform. It is then put back in its cage, safe. After a few trials, rather than struggle along the edges, the rat swims directly to the platform.

The rat is returned to its cage.

Then, the scientists fill the pool to cover the platform and add a milky substance to the water, such that the rat loses orientation by visual cues. The rat must safely navigate to the platform for release.

Despite the changes to environment, rats swim right to the platform.

ooooo

I ask my nephew Justin, "What happened?"

"What do you mean what happened?"

We are sitting in my sunroom. He has been living with me for months now. No one else will take him.

"Oh, you want to know what *happened*."

"What went wrong?" I ask.

Our stories are porous, they are igneous rocks.

ooooo

My mother says to me, "Your sister was so good." She pulls down an electric carver. "Every Christmas and Thanksgiving, your sister would come over here and ask to use this carver. She's the only one who's ever used it. She was so talented!"
This is the way memory works for my mother.

My dead sister had only returned to San Antonio for a few years, and time expands to make it seem like a lifetime.

ooooo

The Pied Piper lured the children away because the townspeople refused to pay him.

ooooo

At my dead sister's funeral, she didn't have a single friend there. Not one person to account for camaraderie, her generosity, her everything.

Instead, the pews were filled with immigrants: my parents' friends and Raul's whole family. The service was in Vietnamese, and even dead, she looked beautiful in my *áo dài*.

∞∞∞

The Morris water maze measures a rat's cognitive flexibility.

∞∞∞

Going through my dead sister's jewelry, I give my mother back all her jade bracelets and throw away the fake ones.

∞∞∞

The rat stands on its little platform, like Beauty waiting for Prince Charming's arrival. Oceanic cream surrounds it. The rat chirps to be saved. She is singing.

In Vietnam, my aunt leans over and says, "Take notice of our oxen. They are strong and well fed." And then we cross the border into Cambodia and my aunt says, "Now look at the Cambodian oxen. They are malnourished and poor. That's how we were before and now we are rich." She lifts her hands in thanks towards the cloudless Cambodian sky.

When he left, he said, "I love you." He hugged me from the passenger seat and got onto a plane that took him to a bus that crossed into Canada. Across the border, our old friends were waiting to drive him back to Kingston. I didn't release my seatbelt, but our embrace was not without warmth. It contained eight years, and I didn't even get out of the car. Eight years was long enough.

I cried during the forty-five minute drive home.

I texted Dorothy, "Chris left."

I texted Dorothy again, "I just took him to the airport."

And, "This is not a joke, LOL not LOL."

Still in awe, I went to Dorothy's house, and there, we celebrated the end of a terrible relationship.

Because this is how it all ends: with brutal resentment.

∞∞∞

If I hadn't failed my parents, I would be a medical doctor. I imagine this Other Lily, wonder if she'd be my size or trimmer or fatter, if she'd have bad skin like me, a head full of white hair like me, if she'd do something as shameful as smoke cigarettes. I imagine her friends. Would they look like mine? Does she dress like me? No, I decide, she doesn't. She would succeed in all the ways I have failed. She would not be a professor. She would not be divorced. She would be a good daughter.

∞∞∞

My dead sister's life became a catastrophe and then she died and passed the baton of destruction to her oldest son Justin. She gave him her addiction and her confidence game and they both have had their skin rubbed clean, worn Texas Department of Corrections uniforms, were assigned an inmate number. They both served their time. Justin has been in and out of jail and prison and Rehab for Felons since his mother died. It's been nearly three years. "It's like it's become normal or something," he says to me. "Mayyyyn, that shit should never be normal."

This time, he's kicked the brown and his attitude is bright.

Tomorrow, he's moving back in with me.

ooooo

I had wanted to be a good wife, and for the most part, I was, but the fact that my marriage was a catastrophe doesn't change. Nor was it entirely my ex-husband's fault, but yes, he was crazy and violent and abusive. And then it was over.

ooooo

Inside his dead mother's Gucci fanny pack, among the debris and trash Justin abandoned in my room after the first time he left New Mexico because he couldn't score, I found used syringes, a bent spoon; the whole room smelled of burning.

I had given him my room and I slept in my study—because my selflessness is a flaw I inherited from my mother. I suffer very well; my altruism can leave bruises.

ooooo

He's been gone nearly four years now and we are divorced, and now I pay him alimony.

When he left, he said, "I love you."

And, "If I need it, can you help me out?"

I said, "Yes."

I thought, "I'll say anything, please, just go."

Then came the day that he wanted to make it legal—stipulated—and he doesn't claim his trust fund in the paperwork and I don't mention it either.

He's an anarchist, radically ethical, a feminist. He cares about Indigenous rights.

His dissertation—if he ever finishes it—is on utopias.

Here I thought he would have more integrity than to take money from a woman of color.

He calls it feminism.

∞∞∞

Dorothy texts, "LOL #AnarchistAlimony." She is talking about the book I need to write, my memoir.

∞∞∞

After his first battle rap, we are hotboxing my car with a friend he just met. Justin tells this stranger, "She's kind of like my mom now."

Weeks later, he says to me, "I want a family, the white brick fence or whatever. Don't you want to be a grandmother?"

∞∞∞

Chris forced me to be more responsible, more adult—to take care of him.

∞∞∞

Stability, I learned, is necessitated by fear.

∞∞∞

Weeks when even my cat is too much responsibility for me.

∞∞∞

Mother to a twenty-four year old with addiction and a dead mother. We are all damaged.

∞∞∞

In his lyrics, I recognize myself, in his guise.

∞∞∞

When I was a wife, I ate three meals a day. We ate organic everything. Chris thought salt was unhealthy, so we took our food unseasoned. Now, I eat once a day to lose weight. Somehow, I am healthier, too.

Or, at least I am happier now.

∞∞∞∞

At my dead sister's funeral, Justin's biological father came up to me, called my sister his wife; he said he can be a father to Justin now. He said his son was his responsibility. I looked at this man's face. It's ugly and sun-worn, tired and addicted. I remembered him putting a twelve-inch chef's knife against my sister's throat. Justin was just a baby, and I couldn't have been more than ten. We were both crying and screaming, but Justin didn't understand what was happening.

Yesterday, Justin called me hysterical, begging me to buy him a ticket back to New Mexico. His father and his whole family have failed him, again.

∞∞∞∞

Responsibility, health, double-knotting the laces of your boots before pulling.

∞∞∞∞

Once, there is a village and it is very peaceful. The people in the village are happy and every night there would be a dance in the town square where children would run rosy circles and teenagers would sneak quick wet kisses when adults turned their heads. But menace lurks just beyond these poorly fortified walls.

One morning the villagers rise with the sun as they always do and walk out to greet each other as they always do, and in the middle of the town square is a body—and it was lifeless! The throat had been ripped open, as if by massive jowls. The next morning, another body. And another.

Finally, after nearly ten moons have crested and fallen, a brave man steps forward and it is decided that he will venture into the forest without fear and capture the white tiger who did this.

But how did they know the tiger was white?

The brave man has a family, and he kisses them good-bye, promising a swift return and a new tiger skin blanket to keep them warm during winter shows. "Shhh, shhh," he whispers to his wife. "I am the best marksman in the village." He puts a large hand around the base of her neck and pulls her in for a farewell kiss. She looks away afterwards, as if in embarrassment for the love she feels.

"And you," the man says to his infant son, "you are the man of the house now. Do you know what that means?" But the boy does not. The brave man laughs, gives the boy a quick pet, and leaves.

He never returns, but the white tiger stops killing villagers, and so everyone forgets, except the boy and his widow mother.

Many years later, the boy becomes a young man. His whole life he has trained for only one task: to kill the white tiger who killed his father.

Every year on his birthday, the young man asks his mother for permission to hunt the tiger who killed his father and every year his mother does not allow it. Finally, on the morning of his fifteenth birthday, the young man pleads, and there is a whining cadence to his voice that his mother remembers from infancy. *Would it be different*, she wonders, *if he had actually had a father?*

"Your father," she says, "could shoot a tin can filled with water off my head from a mile away and not spill a drop."

The young man fills a tin can with water and places it on his mother's head. He paces out a mile and turns around. His eyes are clear and his aim is taut, but he misses the can entirely. Recognizing his error, he begins to train again.

For three years, the young man works and he works and he struggles. Then, he says to his mother, "I am ready." Again, he fills a tin can with water and places it on her head. Again, he paces out a mile and turns around. This time, he takes a breath. He points the gun and shoots.

Over lunch, the mother says, "I am so proud of you, son. Your father would be too. Your skill has nearly met his."

The rice she has cooked is perfect: not too sticky, not too dry. She squeezes a wad of it into a tight ball and pops it into her mouth. "Your father," she says, "used to be able to shoot the eye out of a needle from a mile away." She shakes her head. "I wouldn't expect you to be able to do that, but if the white tiger ate your father, he will surely eat you too."

Mother and son go outside. He places a sewing needle against a tree trunk and paces a mile out. He shoots and completely misses, barely makes contact with the tree itself, which to be fair is rather thin.

For three years, the young man works and he works and he struggles. Then, he says to his mother, "I am ready." Again, he places a sewing needle against a tree trunk. Again, he paces out a mile and turns around. This time, he takes a breath. He points the gun and shoots.

The mother looks at the needle. Its eye is perfectly gone. She is joyful and distraught. See: the boy's father was an excellent marksman but he never performed these impossible feats. She made them all up! She had hoped that she had derived such unreasonable tasks that he would recognize his folly, his lack of preparedness, and never leave, but alas, she must admit, "It is time."

ooooo

Other Lily doesn't fail at marriage, and her husband is Vietnamese. He respects her, too.

ooooo

So drastic is the shift in Justin that he seems to have drifted out of Ovid's pages. There was a time, before, when the pupils of his eyes were floodlit with evil. Heroin eyes. They were shiny and vast, oceanic, sublime. And now those same eyes are gentle and caring. He cries from those eyes when his family is cruel to him. He calls me and is no longer ashamed to weep.

ooooo

Catastrophic or not, we reach the same conclusion: Chris is gone: and I am OK, now.

∞∞∞

I've never been a news person. Too much catastrophe. Or, I just don't care enough about anything other than myself.

∞∞∞

But not all stories must end how mine did with Chris. Some stories really do offer ever after's brimming with happiness.

∞∞∞

Other Lily smiles and her teeth are white. She lifts a perfect little Vietnamese cherub. It pushes its small hands playfully against her face. Their skin is pure.

∞∞∞

A year ago, I was still paying Chris alimony. He wrote me an email entailing all the reasons I should take him back. He suggested long-distance polyamory. I understood then the function of alimony: I was paying him not to be in my life.

∞∞∞

Before work, Other Lily listens to *Democracy Now*. She donates money to PBS and NPR annually. She has it set up for automatic pay.

∞∞∞

Justin and I were never close. I don't interact well with children, and by the time I could find a language that might've opened up our communication, he was a brooding, angry teenager. He didn't want to hang out with his nerd aunt, and I couldn't blame him. I assumed

I would never have a relationship with my nephew and I was more or less fine with that. He'd grown into a thug with low hanging pants and gangsta signs. I didn't know him at all.

∞∞∞∞

Other Lily serves her family dinner. She sits down next to her husband. He feeds their baby soft carrots. Little Tommy is making airplane loops around the table.

I am the Little Match Girl standing outside and salivating at all that is not mine.

∞∞∞∞

I would take a million more black eyes and public bruises than the vitriol of Chris's manipulative and demonic words. They wielded power over me. I believed their heinousness, and sometimes, when I am least suspecting, the insecurity he drove into me still rises up to my skin in oil and I break out often.

∞∞∞∞

When Chris emails me, he says he's gone through a lot of therapy and all of his issues are under control now. His privilege—white and all the others too—is mighty. I wish I had that brand of confidence. Instead, I just don't reply.

∞∞∞∞

The young man travels through the village and into the forest and out of the forest and into another village. It sits inside a copse of trees, and the white tiger is known to live just beyond. The village is very small and the man makes his way to its only inn.

The innkeeper is a gentle old crone, and upon her very first glance of this young man knew immediately that he was the son of another very handsome young man who many years before had crossed this same threshold, looking for a warm room and a cold ale. "Many men have travelled here before you," she says. She says, "You are not the first to go hunting the white tiger."

The inn is humble but not tragic. The thatched roof barely leaks and all of the glasses are clean. They shine.

"Once, there was a young man who you resemble greatly, and he was the best marksman I have seen. He could shoot a grain of salt from a distance of three miles, and he did not survive the white tiger. Surely you cannot do this."

The innkeeper and the young man go outside. He places a single grain of salt on a tree trunk, paces three miles, and turns around. He shoots and completely misses. The young man asks the innkeeper for a room.

For three years, the young man has worked and he has worked and he struggles and now he is a man. Then, he says to his innkeeper, "I am ready." This time, he takes a breath. He points the gun and shoots.

"Splendid!" the innkeeper shouts. It is a beautiful day. Sunshine slates the scene with hope. "But," she says, "I remember he also used to shoot a shot so soft it could split a single strand of my hair right on my head and still have the strand remain in tact."

The man is tired. For years now, he has worked and he had worked and he has struggled. Finally, he says to his innkeeper, "I am ready."

This time, the first time, he fires and the shot is so soft that it divides a single strand of her hair without removing it from her head. She sighs and shakes her head. These feats she told the boy she remembered his father doing, well, she had made them up—for she did not want to see another young man fall prey to the white tiger, but still, she says, "It's time."

The man makes his way through the forest. The brush is dense and he has a good number of cuts along his arms and legs, but he is diligent. He will catch this white tiger, this ghost.

Although there are no roads or paths, an old crone woman crosses his way. She is very frail and hungry. The man shares a rice cake with her. "This is a dangerous place, and there is only one reason you might be here." She shakes her head. "Turn around. Go back. You will die in the jaws of the white tiger, I promise you."

Seeing her hunger, the man gives her another rice cake and she continues, "The white tiger is as cruel as lightning and just as fast.

If you see him, you will already be dead. To kill the white tiger, you must catch him from very far away. All you will see is a white dot. The moment you can discern that it is in fact the white tiger, you may as well slit your own throat. That's how dead you will already be." She shoves the last of the rice ball into her mouth and leaves.

The man sits quietly for many hours. He looks into the distance and clocks a map of the mountains and land. He memorizes each fold of the earth, each protrusion. He sits this way for many more hours. Soon, he has sat there for days and weeks pass and he is studying. One day, far in the distance, there is a change. There is a slow movement, a white dot raised against a geography he has blacked into his mind. He raises his pistol, closes one steady eye, takes a breath, and shoots. The landscape becomes stationary once again.

ooooo

Once, pushing her thumb hard against the kitchen table, Chris's grandmother had said, "Sometimes a husband dies," and she lifted her thumb, "and the widow just blossoms." Her hands shot out to indicate a bursting forth.

ooooo

At the hospital, Other Lily saves two lives and loses none. This is just another day.

ooooo

Days before I find his mother seizing on the ground, days before she dies, Justin and I share a blunt and suddenly we are friends hot-boxing his mom's garage. He shows me Gia Medley and we nod our heads to Kendrick Lamar.

And then his mother died: when he was addicted to heroin, he would text me and I would try to ignore it for as long as possible. I knew he needed me to wire him money immediately. It was never much. He wasn't greedy. Just enough to score. Forty here. Sixty there. His car ran out of gas too many times.

Three years later, he is living with me and clean. Caution signs strobe against my optimism.

∞∞∞

The other day over milkshakes, my friend Thomas tells me he had an "encounter" with Chris. He indicates the scare quotes with his fingers. In my head, I am freaking out that maybe he's come back into town and what if he tries to see me and what if he comes by the house and what will he do. It's not that I'm scared for my safety, but I am.

Chris, it turns out, started following him on Instagram.

"I think it's to see if there are pictures of you on my Instagram," Thomas says. "And there are. A lot."

I push at my lemon pie milkshake. It's late summer, but the evenings are cool in the desert. There's a strong wind and it blows the napkins off our table.

"So I clicked on his Instagram." Thomas is silent for a minute, waiting for me react. There's a childishness to him, an eagerness to please.

Relieving him, I say, "And what'd you find?"

"Mostly just pictures of him and his parents."

"Hm."

"Wait, unless he's just hanging out with people who look like his parents."

"Are they fat and white, vaguely miserable looking?"

"Yes."

"Those are his parents."

"Oh, and there's one with him next to a sports car, pretending like it's his."

Thomas, like all my friends, hates Chris. They remember the way he devastated me, not in his departure but during his presence.

"Chris doesn't have a sports car."

"Do you want to see them?" Thomas pats at his pockets. "Shit, it's charging in the car."

I don't want to see the pictures. I don't want to see Chris. Even a picture is too close.

∞∞∞

My friend Dylan says, "What's the catastrophe today, Lily?" We are eating orange tofu, and Dylan shakes his head every time I mention my boyfriend Harold. All of my friends, even the most patient and diligent, now urge me to end things, take care of myself, first. Mostly, they are sick of my obsession with Harold. They are sick of my sadness.

When we text about it, we call it Tofu Belly.

∞∞∞

Other Lily is out with her girlfriends. They clink their martini glasses and wink flirtily at each other. Men hit on Other Lily, but she is not the type to stray. More than loyal, she is in love. And all her loyalty and love is reciprocated, an equal distribution of desire and faith.

∞∞∞

Laughter cued like clockwork.

∞∞∞

Later, in the car, Thomas pulls out his phone and starts jabbing at the screen. "Weird," he says. He says, "What other screen name would he use? He's not under Chris." He controls the screen by moving his index finger up and down. When he lifts his finger, I see colors carousel like lace tracers. "I knew it."

"What?"

"He just added me to see your pictures. He's not following me anymore."

"Why would he add you on Instagram just to look for pictures of me when he can just Google image me?"

"Duh." Thomas has a way of inflecting tone that perfectly matches his emotion. It's aggravating and endearing. "It's not the same thing."

I agree. It's not.

∞∞∞

I have no idea where Chris is now or how he is. I wrote him an email more than a year ago and he never wrote back. I told him I was going to stop sending spousal support. He was supposedly starting grad school again after taking a year to *psychologically heal* from the *damage* I *inflicted* upon him, and grad school carries with it a stipend that surpasses the annual income supported by our marriage settlement agreement. Furthermore, he has a trust fund.

I hope he finds relief in his anger, I honestly do.

∞∞∞

The man walks a distance of five miles to reach the white tiger. It is a large beast, and its white is unadulterated. He touches it. Its fur is subdued against the enormity of the thing itself. As his hand passes its ribs, he feels a knocking. Then he hears cries for help, muffled and distant and clearly distressed. He opens the white tiger's mouth and climbs in. Inside, it is wet and dark, but there is only one clear path, and so the man makes his way into the white tiger's belly.

By the time the man reaches an opening, he is fully soaked in mucous and blood. A beautiful girl runs towards him. She is stunning in that way that silences a man. "You've saved me! You've saved me!" She throws herself into his chest.

"What's this?" a voice calls from a dark crevice. "Are we saved?"

The man whose voice had just called stands up. He uses the white tiger's intestinal lining for support. He is not old but he is not so young anymore either. The man who used to be a boy looks at this other man and sees in him a resemblance so keen as to be unmistakable. Yes, this was his father. The two embrace with the warmth of a sun flare.

The son returns his father to their home, and when his mother sees their approach, her screams contain uncontainable delight. Over dinner, his mother learns that the beautiful girl is the daughter of the king's highest counselor, and tomorrow, her son must bring her to the palace to reunite their family.

The son rarely returns to his house in the village now that he is married to the beautiful girl. The king, seeing in the man a bravery and skill unmatched by any other before him, makes him commander of the army. They are terribly happy, to this very day.

As for the man and his wife, tonight, they sleep under the warmest white tiger fur blanket in all the lands.

ooooo

I am Justin's only family now.

ooooo

I was not some victim though. Our relationship was a map of hurt, and its scale was strictly emotional.

ooooo

Face the facts: there is no Other Lily, and I'm pretty satisfied with my life.

ooooo

Once, the tiger's wife became very ill. Although they lived in the wild, the tiger travelled through many lands to find a doctor who would treat his wife. "Treat my wife," says the tiger, "and I will not eat you." Many times, he had been forced to eat the doctor. And the tiger's wife became more and more ill. Until she died. The tiger was forlorn. He gathered kindling in his mouth, and splinters arched into his gums and tongue, but he pressed on.

Her funeral pyre was blazing. Taken with grief, the tiger joined his wife in silence. There were no grand trumpets, no cries of despair. Real sadness does not need a performance. He placed his body around hers, holding her gently amidst wild waves of fire. In the smolder of morning, the wind flitted away swirls of ashy particles and an incandescent white tiger stepped forward.

on MEASUREMENT

SPRING

Chinese New Year begins in the spring.

ooooo

When I lived in Indiana, we neither sprung forward nor fell back. We stayed completely stationary while other states moved time without us.

ooooo

Damsels, suspended in time, waiting—shhh, shhh, my princess—because Charming is due to arrive when the snow fades from white to brown and primary colors begin to peek from the months of burial—right on cue.

ooooo

Some music scholars argue that Vivaldi's *Four Seasons* are sonnets. Music scholars argue Vivaldi was a poet himself.
   I scan the score for iambs.

ooooo

The Gregorian calendar was proposed by Pope Gregory XIII in 1582. The New Year was moved to from spring to winter; leap years were calculated to the fourth decimal point.

ooooo

But spring is an awakening. All that has been dormant wakes, as though Charming has pumped life through these limp bodies. Buds push their way through sleeping branches like birds know to begin their migration north when days commence in their elongation.

ooooo

Music following a metronome that counts downbeats.
    There is no downbeat in words, no time signature, just a series of accents that imitate an unwavering tick.

ooooo

The pendulum clock was invented in 1656, and time learned some consistency.

ooooo

Leap years are divisible by four.

ooooo

The academic year begins in the fall when no other calendars begin there.

ooooo

The stars say the year begins in the spring, with Aries.

ooooo

Time, by Papal decree.

ooooo

With only a pedestrian understanding of animals, I didn't know a ram is a male goat.
    The way its horns spiral.

ooooo

I have four apps on my phone for horoscopes. I check the Internet, too, to see if stars can be interpreted the same way. I pick the most optimistic one and hold it close.

ooooo

Celestial time.

ooooo

Once, there is no time, just thick ripe vines and thorns that form a ruthless obstacle course. When Beauty wakes, spring opens her eyes, too, and time rushes forth—and does she retain her beauty now that she is old? Will Charming still love her?

ooooo

Lunar time.

ooooo

Any five consecutive months—excluding February and all her wackiness—contain 153 days.

ooooo

Feminized time.

ooooo

The tree shakes its leaves and down falls a dress made of new emerald leaves. It sparkles under midnight bells.

ooooo

Un-feminist time.

Time must be taught. It's confusing.

○○○○○

There is no variable for time in physics.

○○○○○

The unit for solar time is the day.

○○○○○

Although its math is precise, time has the texture of magic.

○○○○○

Greece didn't accept the Gregorian calendar for centuries, but in 1923, the state relented.

○○○○○

Without a leap, it's called—*common.*

○○○○○

Time standardized for trains and later for the bombs of the Great War.

○○○○○

I played the second movement of "Winter" my sophomore year of high school. An articulation of loneliness, sound compressed and released my desolation.

○○○○○

Before, you boarded a train London and arrived in Paris without synchronicity. It could be any time at all.

∞∞∞

Largo is defined as a direction. Its slow movement, 40-60 beats per minute.

∞∞∞

Snow White has only known spring.

∞∞∞

The human heart pounds softly against the ribs at 60-100 beats per minute.

∞∞∞

Andante versus largo.

∞∞∞

Beauty's heart beginning to beat: from 0 to 60 to a blissful ever after.

∞∞∞

But in his score, Vivaldi marked the second movement of "Winter" andante, which is 76-108 BPM.

∞∞∞

Time by rotation: of the moon like uniform cogs.

∞∞∞

Winter used to be faster.

Under the Julian calendar, a year lasted 365.25 days. According the Gregorian calendar, the year was only 365.2425 days long, reducing the year by ten minutes, forty-eight seconds.

In Spanish and Italian, his name is not Charming but the Blue Prince.

Up to 68 beats per minute faster: a whole heartbeat's worth of time.

The Common Era or Current Era or Christian Era: time measured through religion.

Time neglects to honor Eastern traditions, where time moves in animals, crossing the line of their Great Race.

Composed around 1720, the Gregorian calendar had already been accepted, but *The Four Seasons* revolts, stands in the past, untaught.

When Charming arrives, she is gone. She has already been saved, a season ago. Leaves gather on branches, resolute.

In Port Townsend, reclined in a park overlooking the farmer's market and behind it the ocean, Rikki Ducornet and I eat salmon burgers. She says, "I don't like this boyfriend of yours."

"No one does," I say. And, "But I'm in love."

"Do you really want him in this book?"

There's so much green here: the grass, the trees, the whole Pacific opening into Rikki's serious eyes.

And of course she was right about everything, which became this revision.

One beautiful fall day, there is a rabbit and she is hopping along a stream. She isn't a particularly mirthful rabbit, but she is not dour either. She's just a rabbit, hopping along a stream, on an unexceptional day, an ordinary day. She doesn't ask for much, and she doesn't need much. As she makes her way, she spots a large tiger. She panics. She doesn't know what to do. Her small tail is a puff of gray cotton. The tiger approaches. "Oh, woah woah, old sport," the rabbit says. "Where do you think you're going?" The rabbit balances herself on her hind legs, uses her paws to gesticulate.

Tiger has never been spoken to this way before. Who was this rabbit to be talking to him with such a common tongue? "I'm Tiger," says Tiger. "And who, pray tell, are you?"

"Me?" The rabbit leaps and bounces right in front of Tiger's face and bounces back to safety across the river. "I am the King of Rabbits."

Tiger has never met any kings before and is suddenly nervous. To compensate, he says, "You may be the King of Rabbits, but you're not King of Tigers."

"I fail to see how this is relevant because you, sir, are here, standing in front of the King of Rabbits, and if you want to pass, you will need to pay a tax."

Rabbits are known for their cunning. There's something inherently untrustworthy about those long velveteen ears.

"Wait," says Tiger, suddenly suspicious. "Why should I believe you're the King of Rabbits? Prove it."

The rabbit laughs. "Do you think I have it printed on my driver's license or something? Wait, I think I might have a business card handy—I'm a rabbit! I'm the King of Rabbits!" The rabbit, at the point, is jumping up and down wildly. Tiger can barely focus on her. Of course, Tiger does not know the rabbit is a girl, that she cannot, in fact, be king of anything: even her blood is provincial. "OK, fine. Let's do this. Let's just have a little contest and I'll show you how much greater I am than you. Would that prove to you that I am the King of Rabbits?"

They decide that jumping should be the first contest. When Tiger lines up to jump, the rabbit grabs a hold of his tail, and as Tiger jumps—and jumps far!—the rabbit uses the tail's momentum to fling herself even further forward. Whereas Tiger was pleased with his jump, its grace and distance, pleasure is quickly replaced with awe when he sees the great length at which the rabbit had jumped. It exceeded his jump many times over! Tiger's confidence drops. Suddenly, he is worried he has upset the King of Rabbits. He has challenged his (her) authority and made him (her) compete in this stupid contest, which, surely, Tiger would lose.

The next contest, they decide, should be vomiting. Now it has been days since Tiger has eaten, but he still manages to force some water out. The rabbit, on the other, releases a voluminous heap of tiger fur with a single croak. The rabbit chuckles, winks at Tiger, and says, "Last night's dinner."

She winks, again.

And Tiger takes off running into the woods.

Tiger runs with such blind momentum that he runs right into a fox. The fox says, "Hold your horses there, Tiger." They are, it seems, friends.

Tiger is breathless and panting. He says, "The King of Rabbits is down there. He's going to kill me."

The fox laughs. "Tiger, you silly," she fluffs her tail up in Tiger's face. She is, it would seem, flirting. "I can't believe a rabbit scared you like that. Aren't you supposed to be King of the Jungle or something?"

The fox convinces Tiger that they should go back, and Tiger, knowing that the fox is not nearly as brave as she makes it out to be, ties their tails together, lest she run away in cowardice.

Meanwhile, the rabbit is taking a nap. She is so very exhausted from all her adventures today, and just her luck, the moment she shuts her eyes, she hears a commotion: the fox and Tiger are trying to sneak up on her but are still some distance away. She sits up, alert. Her vision is clear, and her brain is parsing out an equation for survival. She bellows out to these carnivorous beasts, "Well hello there, dear fox, what are you dragging by the tail for me today? What is that? A little dog?"

Realizing he's been duped, Tiger takes off at full speed back into the forest, dragging the fox along with him, all the way back to the little cottage he calls home.

ooooo

According to the Chinese, it is the rabbit who crosses the finish line to the Great Race next. According to the Vietnamese, it is a humble house-cat. Which, pray, tell, is the more heroic, the more deserving of an entire year dedicated to her?

It's my final morning in Iowa. I have spent the past four weeks teaching a fiction workshop on magic. There is barely any snow left on the ground and the sun has not yet risen. This afternoon will be warmer, but I will already be gone.

ooooo

To ward off a winter of depression, I bought hundreds of dollars of yarn and knit cowls for all my friends. Knitting, I felt manic and desperate and then finally calm. My fingers looped yarn, and something solidified, quickened into something else.

ooooo

Cornell College supplied me with an old Victorian house, gabled and ivied, as if straight from a fairy tale. The wood below my socked feet groaned at every step, and ghosts are only imagined in stories.

ooooo

On the first day of class, as an ice-breaker, I had my students play Light as a Feather, Stiff as a Board. In small groups, students huddled around another student who was lying on the ground, perfectly stationary. Using just two fingers to lift, they chanted, "Light as a feather, stiff as a board, light as a—" and I walked around and saw nothing happen.

"You have to believe," I chided. "You're not believing!"

And the students chanted, "Light as a feather, stiff—" and still nothing was happening. This was no surprise to me. It shouldn't work.

Outside, snowflake ballerinas spun and they spun.

I said, "Come on, guys, you have to at least try!"

The students chanted, "Light as a feather, stiff as a board," again and again—until: a girl began to lift off the ground. Her classmates' fingers barely touched her. She was rising, as if effort and determination alone could bring forth magic. I looked over and the other group was standing and their girl was floating nearly waist high.

The students re-arranged the tables and returned to their seats.

ooooo

I call a thing "magic" if I cannot immediately understand the process by which it is made, like electricity and felt, happily ever after and swamp coolers in the desert, like discrimination and cruelty, like the residual buzz that rattles in the small of your ear when all you should hear is silence, like a threat.

ooooo

"How did that work?" I asked. "That's not supposed to work."

The students' faces were bright, celebratory.

"I mean, physics tells us that you can't lift a whole adult person off the ground using a couple of fingers and some chanting." The heater kicked on, and its low warble invigorated me. "It's just not possible!"

I had an entire lecture planned around why the exercise hadn't worked: about how we as adults are too skeptical to believe in magic; about how we put all of our faith in science, which not too long ago was also a form of magic; about how we're cynical and that's sad; about how we can no longer access childhood wonder.

My entire lecture was obsolete.

I let the class out an hour early.

I did not need to convince them, because they already believed.

ooooo

Still without sun, the sky begins to lighten. This is my favorite time of day, just the watching. As if using vision for the first time, these colors absolve everything. In a few hours, I will leave here and I want to say I'll leaved her changed, but I haven't. But at least I made it to the end.

ooooo

I taught fairy tales and myth and magical realism and just plain magic. Students wrote stories of the travails of shape-shifting foxes, the housing of damaged souls, eternal return.

ooooo

Round 1: *yo, sl2, k1, p2sso, yo, k3, rep from * to end.
Round 2: Knit.
Round 3: *k3, yo, sl2, k1, p2sso, yo, rep from * to end.
Round 4: Knit.

ooooo

I took pills to keep me alert, to push aside sleep in order to finish my critiques in time for workshop. I put little hearts next to beautiful passages and across their pages I drew squares around my marginalia.

I read my endnotes verbatim because I have never had the confidence to speak without clear talking points.

I said, "Once is an accident, twice a coincidence, three times a pattern."

I said, "If there's a rifle over the mantelpiece in the first act, it needs to be fired by the third."

My students wrote down every aphorism and nodded their heads.

ooooo

I took a guess and pronounced it incorrectly. It took her two tries to guess that I was trying to say "cowl." "Oh," the lady at the yarn store said, and I said, "Oh," and felt incredible shame.

ooooo

On *The Autobiography of Red*, a student said, "This book was a waste of my time," and I caged my violent desires inside me.

ooooo

A loneliness that might as well shove you into the snow and leave you there, broken.

ooooo

The wind, its savagery and its wrath.

ooooo

I want to hold time in my fists, I want to remember this.

ooooo

My students sewing books as coffins of memory.

ooooo

The weekends here make me desperate. Alone with myself, its jarring solitude and quiet. Snow melting. The dimming of noises, I am only my knitting bones.

ooooo

What is tense—that slippery beast—I purl and then unpurl, counting stitches in multiples of four.

ooooo

For two winters now, Harold has broken up with me and we have mended. He is sometimes cruel to me, sometimes delicate, as though I were an exquisite thing.

ooooo

My ambivalent desire: survival.

My house was dry and it felt like summer in there, but outside, winter continued to bloom.

I unstitch the real and out tumbles magic.

Genesis and *The Odyssey*, we read Bernheimer and Calvino.

I've made my bed every morning: it's the little things.

Grimm and Ovid, we read Borges and Kafka, too.

Some nights I fell asleep with every light on. I couldn't reach the lights. I was crawling along the floors with exhaustion.

Winter, deep in my bones.

The Iowa sunrise, the pink sky: I'm captivated.

on my BIRTHDAY, DRAGONS, AND INTESTINES

Today, I turn thirty-three, the year of Christ.

ooooo

My parents are devout Catholics. Before she is my dead sister, she is a perfect failure of a daughter. And then she is dead. To Christ, they ask why.

ooooo

My dead sister's son puts heroin through is body. He called it the dragon.

ooooo

He doesn't remember it's my birthday, so Harold says, "Did you know today is national sarcasm day?"

Because I am too unstable, Harold is no longer my boyfriend. Now, he's my lover, and I still drive 800 miles each way every month to see him.

ooooo

When all of social media remembers.

ooooo

My hypochondriac mother on odysseys to explain sadness, because it must be something physical. Until her insides push outward: uncontrolled liquefied shit: while driving, in stores, not quick enough to the commode: its stain and its stink.

ooooo

Of course, Facebook has reminders. That's easy.

∞∞∞

Cancer doesn't explain my mother's sadness, but they prescribe her SSRIs all the same.

∞∞∞

They prescribe her medical marijuana pills because her appetite is so bad, because her body rejects comfort. When I tell her what they are, she throws them in the trash. "Drugs," she says. She says, "Bad," both words in English.

∞∞∞

I write a story in which I list out my parents' prescriptions—the battle of journals to publish my Asian American plight.

∞∞∞

The word "medicine" in Vietnamese translates as "drugs": Tylenol or weed, Oxy or meth.

∞∞∞

I disgust.

∞∞∞

This essay already feels too honest, but I'll publish it anyway: I am not worth a nickel of shame.

∞∞∞

My dead sister's son, I can't imagine how the cessation of dragons feels, their slow extinction, his fall.

ooooo

From one map comes others, centuries ago, saying, "Here there be dragons," at the edges of our flat world, but there were never any dragons.

ooooo

Is it bad that I keep checking Facebook and Twitter, counting up the good tidings for a birthday that portends death and resurrection?

ooooo

My mother on the edge of the world, hardly surviving.

ooooo

I remember—the shadowing of her skin, how warmth to her felt like ice—the perpetual motion machine of my excuses for my absence.

I couldn't handle my mother's sickness. It wasn't fear of contamination. I was just afraid.

ooooo

Bhanu, writing me a letter that will become a book about the rape of a woman in India. The woman's intestines were mashed up with a metal pipe.

ooooo

My father smokes a pipe. Daily, my mother warns him of cancer, using her own body as scientific evidence.

ooooo

The day my sister dies, I go on my first date with Harold. There is a certain weight to this, a significance. Now it has been nearly three years and when he breaks up with me, he always says, "You don't love me. You just like our story." He says, "We're not even compatible. What do we have in common?"

∞∞∞

It's too cold for me to be writing outside, but I like the view. I can only smoke outside.

∞∞∞

He says, "I want to get married some day," but not to me. He says, "How can I meet the woman of my dreams if I'm in a relationship with you?"

∞∞∞

Here I am, 800 miles away from home, in Harold's apartment, turning 33 alone.

∞∞∞

The number of times my ex-husband called me a liar, exponentiated by my already low self-worth. And so I believed him.
     Am I really a liar? I'm not sure.

∞∞∞

The geography of my house in Dorothy's poetry, we are the intestines of my house, bringing it mirth and smoke.

∞∞∞

Imagine the dragons.

∞∞∞

A doctor draws me a picture of my sister's heart. He shades a valve, explains how it's vegetation, that there's no real cause and her situation can only yield one conclusion.

∞∞∞

My brother was supposed to be a doctor. He was getting a MD/PhD in neuropharmacology. Then he quit. Then he trimmed. Now he marathons.

When I visit, my father says, "He needs to go to Vietnam and get a good wife."

He married his husband last month.

Every expectation my parents had for their only son gets transferred onto me.

∞∞∞

How many versions of this essay will I save? Command Shift S.

∞∞∞

I am supposed to be a doctor. This is the immigrant parents' dream and I am its failure.

∞∞∞

If not a doctor, my mother suggests: diplomat, dentist, pharmacist, doctor.

Being a professor is not enough.

Being a writer is an indulgence.

∞∞∞

Smoking and birth control mean an increased chance of blood clots.

∞∞∞

On *Game of Thrones*, I predicted, "Once a dragon appears, it's game over."
I was wrong.

ooooo

My nephew tells me how much weight he's gained, now that the hero
has slain the dragon.

ooooo

Harold burns below my skin, and I become sad again.

ooooo

A sadness that pervades, an effusive sadness.

ooooo

Harold and I remove the shells from crawfish and eat their innards. In
less than a week, we have put a dozen of their pounds into our mouths
and swallowed. He wears a bib because he is messy and I wash my
hands twice and they still feel gritty.

ooooo

Half my life I refused my body of meat.

ooooo

To my parents, my dead sister is pure because they have forgotten how
she blew damage into our bodies like fire.

ooooo

My own dragons of escape.

ooooo

To my mother, *borderline* means Forrest Gump. That is not the same *borderline* as my dead sister.

∞∞∞∞

I am afraid because my dead sister and I are too similar.

∞∞∞∞

I chose Notre Dame to appease my Catholic parents, to make them proud.

∞∞∞∞

My parents understand *currency*.

∞∞∞∞

I odyssey for Princes Charming to save me, diasporated anywhere but where I am.

∞∞∞∞

Patronymic: alone: second generation diaspora.

∞∞∞∞

Suddenly, I have a fetish for long distance relationships.

∞∞∞∞

I am probably less damaged than I feel right now.

∞∞∞∞

Our marriage counselor looked me right in the face and asked if I deserved it and then I ended up agreeing with Chris that, yes, it was all my fault, I was a liar, it was all my fault, yes, especially the sweltering bruise blasting around my right eye.

ooooo

Dorothy keeps insisting I need to write a memoir: *Anarchist Alimony*. "Boom," she says, laughing.

ooooo

I have never hated anyone before, and now I know an entirely new emotion.

ooooo

This may not be exactly how it happened, but Chris was on a one-way flight back to Canada less than twelve hours later no matter how I rewrite these moments of precipice.

ooooo

I may be a liar, but I maintain the honor of my words.

ooooo

My bank's overdraft fees rush me until I am tackled.

ooooo

Bhanu and I collaborate on essays about punctuation, the body, desire, shame: post-colonial everything.

ooooo

My lover doesn't have a trashman. He has a trash valet.

ooooo

At least there is the cultural capital of being a professor.

∞∞∞

My mother's colon is the problem. A decade of remission, and it is still in the present tense.

∞∞∞

Selah periodically saying, "My dead mother," the way I write, "My dead sister."

∞∞∞

Dorothy and I write a book together. It is not about our dead sisters, but now that they are dead, what isn't about them anymore?

∞∞∞

My mother doesn't tell me that doctors have called her back in for polyps on her colon, for their foreboding, until she is already driving to her colonoscopy.

Later, she says, "It hurt this time." She doesn't say, "I'm scared," but we both are.

∞∞∞

Besides heart vegetation, my sister's brain aneurizes, leaks blood. "A catch-22," the doctor says. He looks pleased with his literary reference—because I am an English professor.

∞∞∞

The doctor says, "If she'd taken her blood thinners after they coiled her aneurysm, you know, she'd be OK right now."

∞∞∞

The forks of life: one way she lives, the other takes me to today.

∞∞∞

Heredity is sorority. Like my dead sister, I am a liar.
   I must be.
   Chris said so, too. He said it first.

∞∞∞

I would rather be less high more often than more high right now.

∞∞∞

The catheter they seamed into my mother's chest, better to chemo you with, my darling.

∞∞∞

How many lies have been deleted?

∞∞∞

The catheter my sister kept pulling out: comatose brain, thrashing body.

∞∞∞

How much of this is honest?
   This is my vulnerability.

∞∞∞

My dead sister disemboweled her sons' life insurance, their inheritance, their college funds. She did this when she was still married and perfect, for the sake of addiction and fine Italian purses, drug cocktail dresses.

∞∞∞

Like both my brother and my dead sister, I too have a fetish for Louis Vuitton.

∞∞∞∞

To avoid life, I walk ten miles at midnight along a deserted arroyo. I visit a family of foxes and end at the Rio Grande.

During monsoon season, the river is bold.

Otherwise, its dry riverbed is luminescent, but underneath, water flows. It surges, hidden.

∞∞∞∞

The delicacy of intestines.

∞∞∞∞

When I give this essay to Dorothy to edit, she is a magician, making dry lines into lyrical arcs.

∞∞∞∞

My lies slime out with authorial reliability.

∞∞∞∞

I buy a taser because it isn't safe for me to walk alone. It's a femme fatale, a pale pink that imitates girlhood innocence.

∞∞∞∞

Cat-calls and honks, men in cars following pedestrian me for blocks and blocks.

It isn't safe for me to walk during the day, either.

∞∞∞∞

I'm angry.

ooooo

At the army surplus store, the guy says, "Think about it, OK? If you had to, could you really use a knife? Could you stab an attacker?" I imagine the blade reaching through skin and intestines.

Harold answers for me, and we walk out with matching flashlights.

ooooo

Harold's romantic side buys us matching knick-knacks: blinking bike lights, portable battery packs, t-shirts. I would rather he hold my hand—and remember that today is my birthday.

ooooo

"Today is national sarcasm day, did you know that?"
My friend Jeff says, "Sarcasm is the weakest form of irony."
In class, I add, "Which is the weakest form of humor."
My friend Jackie doesn't understand sarcasm.
I don't understand irony.
This is another lie.

ooooo

Birthday wishes rupture the blackness of my telephone screen. The blare of color, the explosion.

ooooo

The chasm in my father's mouth where a tooth should be.

ooooo

The guilt of our Catholicism, we are martyrs.

Rotting and rotten: spoiled.

The guilt of our Otherness, my father tells me I must be smart and work harder than white people, to gain their respect. "Respect," my father says in English.

The guilt of our difference.

I write this against the landscape of a graveyard. Harold's luxury apartment with a luxury view of a graveyard.

Harold and I look at the gated remains of Howard Hughes in the graveyard adjacent to his graveyard.

My dead sister's grave still lacks a gravestone.

In Harold's graveyard, a simple X in stone.

Our ecstasy.

My friend Sabrina with her perfect beauty calls me from a movie set and we spin hot gossip. She wishes me a happy birthday.

I have never asked any mirror about beauty, my sister having wasted it all before me.

In my essays, I call him Charming and believe I am not beautiful enough, not enough a white princess.

ooooo

My dead sister was as arresting as well as arrested, confidant as a convict.

ooooo

Or just not white enough.

ooooo

A world without dragons, can you imagine?

ooooo

So far, 150 plus Internet people remember today is my birthday and Harold cannot remember in real life.

ooooo

My clothes intestinal spin like viscera with Harold's laundry—their smallness against his largeness.

ooooo

Jackie and I talk about our irredeemable obsessions, obsessions within to make witness.

ooooo

How I wax for Harold and he wanes.

ooooo

Justin calls me from Rehab for Felons to wish me a happy birthday. I count the minutes, trying to calculate how much this call is costing me.

"You doing all right?" he asks.

I put more money on his books because his mother is a dead mother now.

ooooo

The first and only time I talk back to my father, it is a week after his birthday and my brother had bought him an Italian Wedding cake and my sister is nearly dead and mold has spread its rot through and through and my father eats it anyway. I beg him not to eat the mold and its infestation and he says something about an immigrant's constitution and it is the only time I yell at my father.

I throw the cake in the trash.

He finishes his slice, silent.

ooooo

Our people do not disrespect our elders. We never talk back. We never disagree.

ooooo

Submission by age.

Aging.

ooooo

He does not eat his slice in silence. When I say, "Please," he says, in English, "If you care, you live here with me."

ooooo

Dorothy texts me daily, mostly just to touch electronically.

ooooo

The gentleness of Harold's skin, the brashness of his fucking.

ooooo

My search of love, defined as a text message when my plane reaches its destination.

ooooo

My dead sister's clothes in large plastic bins, which I pack into my car and drive across the broad state of Texas and into my closet.
  My brother's unopened closet.

ooooo

Harold is my lover now, but there was a time when there was only him. I miss those days.

ooooo

I justify seeing him because I like our story.

ooooo

And my abandonment issues.

ooooo

Dorothy texts me videos of her children crooning happy birthday. Thank you.

ooooo

My sister is still dead.

ooooo

My father's heart, hiccup and burp. Backstrokes and butterflies.

ooooo

My abandoned Geography dissertation: how second generation immigrants imagine a homeland they've never been to.
  Brilliant, I know, and forsaken.

ooooo

Today I am still not ready for things to end—with Harold and everything else, too.

ooooo

Today I can't walk because it's raining.

ooooo

When I am a child, I tell my father he has a watermelon in his belly.
  My first boyfriend Aaron tells me I have fire in my belly. He puts his hand there. "Too hot," he says, his Adonis smile.

ooooo

Justin spends more than a year in the Texas Department of Corrections to rehabilitate.
  My sister spends five years there; I don't even know why.

ooooo

When I peel pomegranates, tenderness for my ex-husband strikes me like the release of venom.

My nephew writes me letters from prison. He writes me poems. They aren't really for me, but I treasure them all the same.

"This isn't really my jam," Zach says, driving me from Harold's apartment. "Too douche."

When I think of my mother's cancer, shame blushes over me because I escaped from her and her sickness as often as I could.

More than 200 wishes, except his.

If all loves could be so pure.

Finally, I tell him it is my birthday and we eat sushi. We talk about his day at work.

This is my rationing of lies, my diaspora.

I learn the difference between Oriental and Asian in middle school. No one in my family teaches me. The people in my family don't care about political correctness or preferred nomenclatures. Watching *The Real World* on MTV, Pam explains that things are Oriental—e.g. vases and rugs, food—whereas people are Asian. To say a person is Oriental makes them into an object.

∞∞∞

I internalized her words as fact.

∞∞∞

The first Asian women I remember on television are Pam from *The Real World* and Margaret Cho in 1994. They become role models by default. I am in middle school.

When Lucy Liu comes on air in 1997 in *Ally McBeal*, I begin high school and she makes Asian very sexy.

∞∞∞

The Japanese have different types of beauty. For example, *mono no aware*, *wabi sabi*, and *ma*. Beauty is always tied to impermanence.

∞∞∞

The old man at the café tells me I would make an excellent wife, and I am already offended but pretend to accept it as a compliment.

Then, Pete says, "Well, do you want to know why?"

I don't want to engage in this conversation. I don't know where exactly it will go, but I know it's bound to be offensive.

"Because Oriental women make good wives."

"Oriental is a problematic term," I say. I use words like "problematic" because I am an academic and this is how we speak: buzz words and hip plastic glasses.

Pam from *The Real World* wasn't some hero to me, but I really noticed her arrival on screen. By middle school, I had already learned to be ashamed of my Asianness, and to see an Asian woman on a popular show—well—it meant something to me.

ooooo

I was angry that Pam got the least amount of camera time.
  "She's just not that interesting," my brother says. "She's a snore."
  I don't disagree with him because he is older than me.

ooooo

Mono no aware translates as "the pathos of things" or "an empathy toward things" or "a sensitivity to ephemera." A thing's pathos is derived from its transcience.

ooooo

Pam the Harvard medical student, the model minority, she's even got a white boyfriend.
  I wished she could be my mentor.

ooooo

Pathos, the emotional persuader.

ooooo

To share.

ooooo

Just another model minority.

ooooo

"Oriental women—" Pete refrains.

I remind myself to respect my elders.

ooooo

Mono no aware is a fleeting, varying beauty.

ooooo

Maybe it was Pam who taught me how to have opinions while remaining unobtrusive. If only we all had diary cams to project into homes with cable television.

ooooo

"And you wanna know why they make good wives?" the old man says.

The courtyard of the café has cleared out. It's almost closing time. Green Christmas lights line the beams.

I light a cigarette and look at him blankly.

"Well, I went to the nail salon the other day and they just really know how to satisfy a man—"

"Jesus, Pete," I say.

ooooo

Mono no aware cannot be captured in a single moment but must be followed through a span of time.

ooooo

It was an action-packed season: that snake Puck gets kicked off and Pedro has AIDS. Pam went to Harvard. She's finishing up medical school. What was she doing on this show?

Fleeting through time.

ooooo

"She makes Asian women look bad," my brother said. "She's so fat. And loud."

My brother was twenty-four and I was twelve when *All-American Girl* came on air. He was in an MD/PhD program in Neuropharmocology. He'd been with his girlfriend for practically a decade. She was Vietnamese, the daughter of a close family friend. I consider her parents my parents too. They consider me their daughter. My parents pretended not to brag about him when they were bragging about him. They loved to brag about him. In a few years, I will be in high school and my brother will quit school and start waiting tables. He and his girlfriend will break up and he will start taking me to gay coffee shops every night. He will exercise maniacally and laugh when people compliment his thinness.

"But she *is* pretty funny," he said.

I also find her offensive, but not for any of the reasons my brother listed. But maybe for those, too.

ooooo

Wabi sabi is a rustic or desolate beauty.

ooooo

Rustic may be charming, but to a Westerner, which I am, there is nothing beautiful about the desolate.

ooooo

Margaret Cho was the only Korean American actor in *All-American Girl*. Not only do all Asians look the same, I couldn't tell the difference, either.

Even at twelve, I expected the show to break stereotypes, but instead it just encouraged them, made them true.

At twelve, I wanted to break stereotypes too, but I didn't know how. So I practiced my violin and did extra math homework every night.

Wabi is an appreciation for things with imperfections.

"What I was trying to say," the old man says, "is that Oriental women make good wives because they know how to cook, how to rub feet, they're pretty, and they don't have opinions."

"OK, Pete, whatever. I used to be a wife and that definitely wasn't the kind of wife I was," I say, except that it kind of was. I feel disgusted—but at whom.

All-American Girl provided me with instructions that I internalized and I didn't even know it was happening.

I am laughing at Pete with some other people at the café. It isn't mean-spirited, but it is. I recount the one where he tells me I'd make a good wife. Everybody laughs.

I say, "Imagine me rubbing his feet!"

Everybody laughs.

My friend Scott is like, "What's the big deal about saying Oriental anyway?" He's an intelligent guy, too intelligent to say something like this. And then my friend Scott is like, "Like Mexican American. Shut up already and just call them Mexican."

On another night, we are playing chess and Pete says, "You know what you'd be really good at?" He's just an obstinate old man, a septuagenarian with a temper and a bad gambling problem. He regularly asks me for a loan, never much, twenty here, sixty there, and he's always good on it.

Then his girlfriend of decades died, and even though it was her dying wish for him to marry her, he wouldn't do it. Now, when he calls me, he leaves me voicemails I never listen to.

"What's that, Pete?"

He has a professional chess set. I love the weight of each piece as I remove it from the board.

"You'd make a great cocktail waitress."

"Thanks, Pete," I say, and I mean it.

⚬⚬⚬⚬⚬

Chris used to tell me that I only got my books published because the guilty white liberals who run small presses wanted me in their catalogue. "They're just using you," he said, "for your name."

⚬⚬⚬⚬⚬

Sabi is rustic or desolate.

⚬⚬⚬⚬⚬

Actually, *All-American Girl* wasn't totally without positive lesson for me: Asian American children can have choice. They can think independently.

Before this show, I didn't know these things were possible for me.

I didn't know independent thinking was an option.

⚬⚬⚬⚬⚬

Independent thinking led me to writing, but if I'd just listened to my parents, I'd be a medical doctor by now.

When I tell Harold this, he laughs and it's malicious. Then, he asks what makes me think I could be a medical doctor. He's like, "You don't even have a doctorate in your own field," and it takes me a minute to understand what he's saying. I hang up on him and when he calls back, he's like, "We must've broken up." He's like, "I mean, our phones broke up, we didn't break up. We're fine, it's just our phones—"

∞∞∞

Wabi sabi is a crude or faded beauty that communes with the dark and desolate sublime.

∞∞∞

Location, location, location. Traditional fairy tales are all about location: namely, nature, frightening nature, it's magical—this *nature*—expansive and haunted, here there be monsters a-lurking and beasts a-creeping, nature is the wildcard obstacle—if the heroine wants to win, that is. In traditional fairy tales, nature takes the shape of the Forest, one if by land two if by sea, as in: the forest Little Red travels through to get to her sick grandmother's house; the oceanic forest the Little Mermaid must navigate to get to the Sea Witch and then to land; the dense thorny vines and deep forest the Prince must crawl and saw through to get to Sleeping Beauty. The Forest is *sublime*: terror-filled rapture, the anxiety of imminent death, the anxious arrival of what comes after. Danger makes the quest—and its prize—worthwhile. But the Forest isn't something to be overcome. It can't be overcome, it's vast and boundless. It's insurmountable. The most that fairy tale characters can do is make their way *through*, or hide. Ready or not.

The sublime forest is obstacle, is obstruction, like a big fucking maze dropped right on the heroine just when things couldn't get any worst. Wait, wait, oh, things *can* get worse: here's this big fucking maze and oh yeah they're in a fairy tale, gee-whiz, insert *magic*. The cherry: she doesn't even have a map, so there goes logic, out the high tower window. Fairy tale heroines may not have maps, but she always makes it to her destination. Think about Snow White: what are the odds that the Huntsman releases her into the woods and she lands with the Seven Dwarves? Think about Hansel and Gretel: in what universe would child abandonment lead to a Gingerbread House? Or consider the probability that Beauty would just—while frantically searching—appear at the very estate where her papa is trapped. Or here's one for you: the Prince questing through the forest of the city to find Cinder's tiny foot.

Logic says the Forest is impossible to navigate, especially without a map or guide.

But that's what makes them heroes and heroines: their ability to intuit their way through the precarious Forest. This is the perk of being good.

∞∞∞

When I tell people I was getting a PhD in Geography, I let them think I am a legit scientist—I revel in their momentary confusion, how impressed they are with me—and then I come clean: it was a total social science: geography of the imagination.

∞∞∞

Three years later, *Ally McBeal* confirms that anorexia is beautiful and so is the exotic.

∞∞∞

I am still trying to impress you.

∞∞∞

In high school, I was awkward and ugly and such a nerd. It was a terrible time.

Because of social media, I now learn from old crushes that they had crushes on me too. I tell them, "Shut the fuck up." I tell them,

"You've got to be kidding me." I tell them, "Impossible." I talk in clichés because I'm so astonished that originality leaves me behind.

ooooo

Beauty must be caught while it is still beautiful—and what happens if it is not.

ooooo

"She's so fierce," my brother said about Lucy Liu.

ooooo

There was no way I would ever be as beautiful as Lucy Liu; I studied harder.

ooooo

There hasn't been a burgeoning of Asian men in film, except in martial arts flicks. When Asian or Asian American men appear on screen, they are smart and effete. White men must shout down because Asian men are small in frame. They must shout to be heard.

ooooo

I have never found Asian men to be attractive. I could blame this on self-hatred or self-shame or an internalization of hegemony, pop culture or personal taste or television. I tell people that I have a white fetish, and everybody laughs. We all agree that I am just plain cute.

ooooo

The old man says he hates bigots more than anything else. "Ignorant," he says. "I just can't stand for that kind of ignorance."

Later that afternoon, he says, "How's your buddy Corey doing?"

There was a time when Corey used to sell Pete a little weed. Then, Pete got into trouble with money and he'd ask for weed on credit and eventually Corey got sick of it. Pete told me he was "psychotic" and they haven't talked since.

"Oh," I say, "he's got a new girlfriend, so I don't see that much anymore."

"You mean a boyfriend," Pete says.

The old man's lost all his teeth. Just last month, my father had to have all his teeth extracted. He's been eating rice porridge every night.

"Come on," he says, "you're the one who told me he's gay!"

"I know for a fact that I've never said Corey is gay."

"We were sitting right over there." He points to a table two tables over. "And we were talking and Corey came up and sat with us, remember?"

He's lost a lot of weight since his girlfriend died. A lot of money, too. He had to get a roommate in order to afford his apartment. He gave the roommate the bedroom and he slept on the couch.

"And I said to him, 'Hey Corey, how old do you think I am?' and he says, 'Thirty-five,' and you said, 'Corey! Are you flirting with Pete?' And—"

"That was a joke, Pete."

"No, it wasn't, because then you asked why he was blushing and why would he be blushing if it wasn't true?"

∞∞∞

In college I was in love with a boy named Jeremiah who was in love with a Japanese girl. She had to move back to Japan and he was forlorn. He would tell me about the purity of their love and our bodies were close enough that I could fool him.

∞∞∞

My assumption, now, is that every man has an Asian fetish.

This is born out of low self-esteem—and fact, it's born out of fact.

∞∞∞

Chris loved my Asian-ness. He made it clear that it wasn't an

Asian thing though. "I just like other women," he said. And to clarify, "Women of color."

ooooo

In the first draft of this essay, I had forgotten about Connie Chung. Connie Chung who exists above petty sexuality and coming of age. Connie Chung, the respected news anchor. I forgot about her.

ooooo

We are so safe we are practically invisible.

ooooo

Practically white.

ooooo

And Harold was like, "You think I have an Asian fetish but I don't," and I was like, "I haven't said anything like that for a long time," and he was like, "But I don't," and I was like, "I know you don't," and he doesn't. He would prefer me blonde with pastel eyes.

ooooo

When he broke up with me the very first time, Harold said, "I would never marry you. You're the wrong color."

Much later, he tells me just said that because he knew it would hurt me. He's not a racist, he insists.

ooooo

Television teaches desire, not just who you should desire but also who you should desire to be.

I line up these powerful Asian American women like playing cards. I compare their stats. Such different women representing such different things. To synthesize these women and blend, to learn: I only had four.

I imagine it must be even more confusing for white women; they have so many to choose from, to confuse, to make you feel inadequate.

Before I ever saw Asian Americans portrayed on television, I watched Chinese serial melodramas. Many of them were period martial arts, but others were romantic and contemporary. I only liked the period films. Men had long hair and women's dresses were both exquisite and functional, and even the women who were the most skilled at martial arts were delicate.

Before there is Metanoia, there is Kairos. He is always before her, in front of her, leading. He is guiding. He is protecting. He never lets her go ahead of him, and it's for her own good. Nascent chivalry and unintentional hard-ons.

Kairos, the god of opportunity, rolls around on his golden ball. Strong wings ripple at his ankles. He is swift. He has a tuft of curls right on the apex of his temple; otherwise, he is fully bald. The lesson being: if opportunity passes by you, you have to grab him by the hair and quickly, before he—and he is gone. Opportunity has passed you by, and who knows if you even noticed.

But luckily, right behind Kairos lurks the shadowy Metanoia, goddess of missed opportunity. She doesn't have a golden ball or spectacular wings. She doesn't even get a horse. No, her fate is to hobble along after Kairos, and to those she deems most worthy, she raises a cloaked hand to reveal a mirror. If you miss Kairos, Metanoia can show you a reflection of yourself, one that might incite change, transformation, a metamorphosis so drastic and necessary that you might surpass the potential of the opportunity Kairos has previously offered. And when Kairos passes you again, later, you will grab his curly tufts and you will pull. You will not watch him roll away.

on VIOLENCE

Once, my father's friend, the Skinny Man, brought over a dead goat. He had hit it with his mini-van. My father helped him bring it in because it was too heavy for one man to carry alone, but they sent me to my room first. I had never seen a real goat up close before and I was excited, even though it was already dead, but I didn't argue. I didn't fight. I was just a kid then, still sleeping with my mother even though I was too old for that. I played house with my marbles; they rolled and sat and drank tea out of tiny plastic pink cups.

Later, the men will drink beer and eat stewed goat.

Later, when I am taking a bath, the Skinny Man will come in and wash his hands, and I will watch how lathering makes bubbles and how quickly the water washes it all away. I will not look at his eyes in the mirror's reflection. The marbles will be slick with soap.

on the GEOGRAPHY OF FRIENDSHIP

FUGUE

... the fear is that the loss of the promising object/scene itself will defeat the capacity to have hope in anything. (Lauren Berlant)

ooooo

For the rest, what we commonly call friends and friendships, are nothing but acquaintance and familiarities, either occasionally contracted, or upon some design, by means of which there happens some little intercourse betwixt our souls. (Montaigne)

ooooo

For friendship is community, and as we are in relation to ourselves, so we are in relation to a friend. And, since the perception of our own existence is desirable, so too is that of the existence of a friend. (Aristotle)

ooooo

... slow and regular friendships... (Montaigne)

ooooo

The death of friends: both memory and the testament. (Jacques Derrida)

ooooo

... friends until that state of profound friendship where a man is abandoned, abandoned by all his friends... (Georges Bataille)

ooooo

All attachment is optimistic, if we describe optimism as the force that moves you out of yourself and into the world in order to bring closer the satisfying something that you cannot generate on your own but sense in the wake of a person... (Lauren Berlant)

ooooo

My complicitous friendship: this is what my temperament brings to other men. (Georges Bataille)

ooooo

Opposition is true friendship. (William Blake)

ooooo

We can, in a word, remember. But thought knows that one does not remember: without memory, without thought, it already struggles in the invisible where everything sinks back without indifference. This is thought's profound grief. It must accompany friendship into oblivion. (Maurice Blanchot)

ooooo

O philoi, audeis philos. (Aristotle)

ooooo

What does friend mean when it becomes a conceptual persona, or a condition for the exercise of thought? Or rather, are we not talking of the lover? Does not the friend reintroduce into thought a vital relationship with the Other that was supposed to have been excluded from pure thought? (Deleuze and Guattari)

ooooo

Love is a desire of contracting friendship arising from the beauty of the object. (Cicero)

∞∞∞

What a shame can there be, or measure, in lamenting so dear a friend? (Horace)

∞∞∞

Some people go to priests; others to poetry; I to my friends. (Virginia Woolf)

∞∞∞

The bird a nest, the spider a web, man friendship. (William Blake)

∞∞∞

Friendship is a sweltering tree. (Samuel Coleridge)

∞∞∞

… knowing how remote a thing such as friendship is from the common practice, and how rarely it is to be found. (Montaigne)

∞∞∞

Before the flowers of friendship fades friendship faded. (Gertrude Stein)

The swarm bellows in a language solemnly exotic to you. You search for cognates and the wind pushes through your skin and through the marrow of your bones and back out. The swarm always returns to itself, changed and whole.

∞∞∞

You are sitting in Brooklyn and people swarm around you. Because of the position of the sun, they are variants of shadow. They are obtrusive and absent stalkers.

You press your hands against the protection of summer glass.

∞∞∞

The smallness of singular objects and the mobs that rise from their accumulation.

∞∞∞

Bees swarm to relocate their fertilized queen to a new home. Not all things require instruction, like: survival and proliferation, instinct and disgust.

∞∞∞

There is a universality to the communication of disgust. Brows and foreheads form gorges. Eyelids grip each other, defiant as an unwanted embrace. Mouths unlatch in an attempt to release, to expel, to jettison and divest.

∞∞∞

In order to join the collective, you must un-become, lose your face and your skin, eject your identity. Then we can emerge uniform, exactly the same, just torso and skeleton. This is called belonging.

Giorgio Agamben's *homo sacer* is expelled from the community. He can be murdered without consequence and Roman gods will not accept him as sacrifice.

You can't imagine a crime that would be justice for this punishment.

∞∞∞

A pack of dogs. A swarm of insects. A mischief of rats.

You desire the human equivalent.

∞∞∞

Kim Hyesoon writes, "my shadows swarm like a pride of lions on the plains / A place where my ashes get up and dance after I've been burnt today."

Her book is filled with swarms: of inserts and attachments.

∞∞∞

You see *homo sacer*'s loneliness in yourself.

You see it in all the people around you, too.

∞∞∞

The disgust of desire.

∞∞∞

To run away is abandonment; it is not the same as being banished.

When you were little, your sister abandoned you. First she ran away from home. Then she went to prison. Your father banished her from the house, but then he let her return. He said he would never love her again. He said she was a tenant. Now that she is dead, there is so much regret.

In *Ban en Banlieue*, Bhanu Kapil writes, "I want the swarming movements mixed with static forms."

ooooo

Desire is striving, the unfulfillment of a mathematical limit.

ooooo

You transform into stone and watch the swarm float on without you. You feel stagnation everywhere in your body, imprisoned.

ooooo

A man can become a myth when he pushes a stone uphill and chases it as it rolls back down. There is no hope for mutation in this story. There is no alternative ending. He never makes it all the way. He never crosses this off his to-do list. And he wants to. He really really wants to. Each minute of his life is filled with intense pushing. It is filled with the hope that perhaps today will be the day he defies the gods again.

His punishment can also be called *eros*.

ooooo

Every morning you write a to-do list by hand to make order out of your day.

You are always too ambitious—and therefore disappointed with your own productivity.

ooooo

If you are allergic and then stung by a bee, wasp, etc., and you don't have an EpiPen: run! Run hard and fast. The adrenaline may not save you, but it could.

Say he does, though, make it up the hill: what then? Would he be stripped of notoriety and be just a mortal once again?

ooooo

Sisyphus was the king of Ephrya, more popularly known as Corinth, but he was not a good king. His crimes included chronic deceitfulness and avarice.

ooooo

You are waiting for Charming to come save you.
    He will come.
    But Charmings are princes and their father is Sisyphus.

ooooo

The swarm is a community. It is to have a place, acceptance. Inside, there is only a beautiful feeling.

ooooo

Nick Flynn writes, "When you see us swarm—rustle of // wing-beat, collapsed air—your mind / tries to make us one, a common // intelligence, a single spirit un- / tethered. You imagine us merely / searching out the next // vessel, anything // that could contain us, as if the hive / were just another jar."

ooooo

From the outside, the swarm is menacing. It is high school all over again: the cliques and popular kids. You live in a liminal space. You don't know what those words mean yet—but you know the emotion that necessitates the naming of things, the creation of new ideas and theories, you intuit what other people spend their careers researching.

ooooo

A flock of birds. A school of fish. A cluster of galaxies, a troop of monkeys.

ooooo

You want language to swarm and eat this carcass you have become until there is only the glint of bone against sunlight.

ooooo

Homo sacer is not merely ostracized. He is banned. He must remove himself from his community.

ooooo

The way you like to imagine you are an outsider.

ooooo

When does otherness dissolve?

ooooo

The swarm moves like tremolo. It ascends with crescendo.

ooooo

What is the swarm? It's a feeling kind of like being in love: of being lifted and carried, thrown into momentum towards—towards—
    Until you are no longer moving forward and you are all alone again and the swarm sinks below your feet; who knows if your heart still works.

ooooo

The swarm of music, its buzz and its sting.

ooooo

Flies cyclone like the dogs' howls congregate.
    It is chilling.
    It is breathtaking.

ooooo

Sylvia Plath writes, "It thinks they are the voice of God / Condoning the beak, the claw, the grin of the dog / Yellow-haunched, a pack-dog, / Grinning over its bone of ivory / Like the pack, the pack, like everybody."

ooooo

You want to talk about desire, the way bodies change—or yours has. The way it could be love or it could be hormones and what is desire and what is yearning and isn't it all just love, that broad umbrella, her stride.

ooooo

A zietgeber is an external or environmental cue that synchronizes an organism's biological rhythms to the Earth's twenty-four light/dark cycle and twelve-month cycle. You lack circadian. Some nights you are dreaming before eight. Others, you watch dawn tint the sky with magical colors only the desert can display.
    Night is a swarm of silence and you wait for revelation.

ooooo

School or hive or swarm, regardless, there were a whole lot of them gathered around your body, huddled and lashing, all that poison and spinning electricity: you glowed in that ocean.

Herd.
It was a herd of Portuguese man o'war.
It was the first time you thought you would die.

ooooo

The swarm is a feeling: of acceptance, of denial, of rejection.

ooooo

The heat of rejection, as bright as memory.

ooooo

You are banished by the swarm, like *homo sacer*, and you will never forgive yourself for the crimes you have yet to commit.

ooooo

The swarm is, after all, your family.

Long before he reached Buddhahood, long before he made such lasting friendships, he was already immortal. Already he had eaten the peaches of immortality. Already he had pissed off the Jade Emperor.

In the present moment, Sun Wukong stands before Buddha, who doesn't look especially at peace. Sun Wukong laughs broadly.

"You laugh now," says Buddha.

Sun Wukong's laughter does not abate, it does not diminish.

"Alright then," goes Buddha. "Let's just put a little money on it."

"Money?" Sun Wukong's face is suddenly very stern. "A man with no possessions certainly can't wager me more than a copper cup!"

"It's just a saying."

Buddha's face is very smooth. He is old but his skin is bright.

"A cliché," corrects Sun Wukong. "You're just a cliché."

But the bet is made nonetheless.

Sun Wukong can jump and far. With one great bound, he leaps to the end of the world. He sees nothing except five pillars. Sure that he has reached the edges of Heaven, he tags the pillars: Great Sage Equal of Heaven. It's his calling card. Or, he pisses on them. He springs forth, but his head hits something hard. A ceiling? In Heaven?

Sun Wukong finds himself cupped beneath Buddha's palm. So lit against shadows, the pillars—it turns out—are fingers. And so Sun Wukong is imprisoned for five centuries.

∞

When I was little, I used to watch Sun Wukong's adventures. They were chronicled as Chinese period soap operas, and they were dubbed into Vietnamese. My favorite part was that he was a human-sized monkey. My second favorite part was his magic staff, which he could collapse into the size of a toothpick and stick in his ear. My third favorite part was his friends: a pig, a water buffalo, and a dragon. They could all change into any animal they wanted. They fought demons and monsters in every episode.

ooooo

In Chinese, his name is Sun Wukong. In Vietnamese, it is *Tôn Ngộ Không*. In English, it is the Monkey King.

ooooo

When I speak with other Vietnamese people, they always applaud my retention of language. The other Vietnamese people say, "Oh, she's so good."

This makes my parents proud and so they say, "She used to watch a lot of Chinese movies."

Days ago, my college roommate called me. "Lils," she said, harkening back to a time of carefree nicknames. Megan exhaled deeply and began to sob. Sometimes we talked several times a year, sometimes years went by without either of us really noticing. I couldn't remember how long it had been since we last caught up, six months? Maybe two years. Her words disjointed into monosyllabic slurs and heaves of slimy breath.

When I finally calmed her, she said, "Johnny's dying."

ooooo

Friendship creates a different valence of space. Friendship, its bond and trust, initiates a shared space that is reliant on a vault of fond memories that can be accessed no matter the physical place or location. Whereas the tangibles of place may not be disturbed, friendship expands like analgesic—until empathy soothes out all the wrinkles.

ooooo

In college, there were six of us: the four girls shared a suite and the boys were roommates. We spent all of our time together. Inseparable, as they say.

ooooo

Alone, I roll over the footage of memories from fifteen years ago. His laughter is the same as a crow's.

ooooo

So much of friendship is tied to proximity and convenience.

Because they betrayed me, I left my friends when I was nineteen, transferred schools and cities, and I thought I'd become a different person, too. That's what happens when you move: you can become anyone you want. I wanted to become strong, feminist, less angsty, more stable—I still want these things.

At nineteen, I was unstable and my friends were worried so they called the cops. We were a group of six and I was being arrested. They were only trying to help. When I think back on the horror and shame and despondency and helplessness I felt in that moment, I push it away and get back to work.

It was betrayal and it was severe but I still didn't think our friendship would fray and dissolve. I thought I'd be angry for a while and then relent and we could press play and continue. This didn't happen though, and I learned that long distance friendships rarely maintain their once lucid urgency. Time passes because it does, and separated friends always make new ones.

∞∞∞∞

Megan and I were put together as roommates our freshman year because we were the only two girls who indicated they smoked on the housing survey. Drunk girls would falter into our room after frat parties to smoke, their little teenaged bodies curling out the window. We both thought it was fate.

∞∞∞∞

Sites of solidarity make my eyes well with nostalgia and hope.

∞∞∞∞

Most of my friends live in places I've only imagined.

∞∞∞∞

The first night we met, Megan and I stayed up all night. I admitted things that I had not told my closest friends and that was how we knew our friendship would be true, long-lasting. I was wrong in some ways, right in others.

That first night, we learned we'd both been raped and I learned that there's a word for fire: feminism. "I'm going to major in

Women's Studies and English," she said, and so I did too. She read her poetry to me and I wanted to write poetry too. She told me about her boyfriend. I didn't have a real boyfriend—I had a guy I wanted to be my boyfriend—but I made him my boyfriend for that night and Megan and I bonded about how hard it was going to be balancing college and boyfriends and love and distance. "We have old souls, Lils."

ooooo

Like the 800 miles between Harold and me.
    Even though I sometimes name him Charming, he is real.
    The ache of separation is real, it hurts.

ooooo

I don't believe in souls, and Johnny Martinez's body will die before mine.

ooooo

Weighted against time, friendship must be balanced; it must be taut. Wires thin over time and a single strand of the strongest wire may bend and bend. Just know that one day it may not be able to endure the pressure exerted on it by immeasurable distance.

ooooo

I have always been desperate to fit in.

ooooo

I have never known anyone dying of AIDS.

ooooo

I am trying to negotiate how to mourn Johnny Martinez. Am I supposed to feel bad about a stranger?

oooooo

A ten percent chance of survival.

oooooo

Pete from the café lands in the hospital. He's a grumpy old man, a curmudgeon and very rude. We used to play chess together every night and then he said one absurd thing too many. I hear a woman say, "I hope he dies in there," and no one deserves that. I don't like the guy, but his crimes do not equal her punishment.

When she says "Hi" now, I ignore her.

I continue typing.

If she sits too close to me, I leave.

oooooo

In between my departure at nineteen and now, I have gone through many incarnations of self. Back when I was still a wife, Chris would ask me what I would've thought of him if I'd met fresh-out-of-high-school punk Chris instead of meeting him in his mid-twenties like I did. He used to listen to Fugazi and be straight edge.

"They're just a little angry for me," I said.

"That's just because you don't have the sophistication to understand their sound," he said. Whereas now I can recognize his tone as defensive and hurt and manipulative and abusive, at the time, even though I'd been a classically trained musician from childhood, I defaulted into believing that he was right.

I contrast that Lily with Professor Lily Hoang, teaching Women's Studies and Feminism. In the classroom, I project confidence and strength. People tell me I intimidate them. This is my favorite Lily to wear.

oooooo

I dye my hair youthful colors: cranberry, turquoise, violet. The color sticks to my white hairs in the unwaning sunshine of the desert.

When the color fades, strangers ask if my grey streaks are real.

ooooo

Johnny Martinez graduated college and lived with our college friends and worked at Whole Foods for a while. Then he got hooked on heroin. Then he got locked up for a significant stint. He was homeless, too. He contracted pneumonia either during prison or shortly after his release and that's what's killing him now.

He's not dying of AIDS. He's dying of pneumonia.

I don't know that guy though. I've never known the person he became, just the person he was when we were still only children making adult decisions and lasting compromises.

ooooo

I want my sadness to be legitimized. I want to be told how to feel.

ooooo

Death devastates, no matter how it happens.

ooooo

My attempt at mourning rings false.

ooooo

I can't stop saying that my friend Johnny Martinez is dying of AIDS. I like to feel the dramatic weight—except that he is neither my friend nor dying of AIDS.

ooooo

Convenient friendships.

My inconvenient relationship with Harold: but how I love the distance and the desire it produces.

"I can't believe this is real," Megan said. Even though it is early spring, I had a fire going.

Like Megan, I wanted to erase reality too, so I walked into a fairy tale where there was no sadness, just sublime challenges and conquests and ogres to defeat.

"Mary Beth said she can't even recognize him."

In the fairy tale, I could be a female Odysseus, woman of many faces.

"I can't believe this is happening."

I could wander around the forest, singing sweet ballads and dancing.

"I mean, how is this happening?"

When will Charming appear? Or will it be the Wicked Old Crone this time?

"I have no idea," I said.

∞∞∞∞

Although I am mourning a stranger, his face is almost familiar.

∞∞∞∞

Friendship, balanced on a scale.

∞∞∞∞

Adulthood: when sisters and old friends die.

∞∞∞∞

Johnny Martinez and I took Ancient Greek together. The class met every day at eight in the morning. There were a total of three students, and Johnny and I ditched at least twice a week. "O Xanthias!" he'd proclaim when he wandered into my room still sleepy. "O Xanthias," I'd mumble in response, and he'd start guffawing and we'd go get high together. Xanthias means blondie. It wasn't a funny joke, just one that we shared.

○○○○○

It's late and I'm looking through Johnny's Facebook profile. Feeling desperate and nostalgic, I click on an old crush's icon and send him a message. His name is Jacob, and I feel pathetic for writing to him at all.

○○○○○

Distance; therefore, distant.

○○○○○

"When he sings it," Johnny said, "he does this thing, 'I'm calling time and temperature just for some company,' and he rolls his eyes up"—Johnny made eyes at me—"and everyone just swoons." He pretended to faint. Later that spring, the Old 97's came to play at our school and when the line careened by, sure enough, Rhett made everyone keel with giddiness and thrill.

○○○○○

We were a group of six and I don't even know where they all live now.

○○○○○

The people in my every day life who don't make it into these essays: why?
    What induces inclusion?

○○○○○

After waxing about Johnny for a while, Megan said, "I'm just really torn, you know, Lil?"
    Megan has recently given birth to her second child. She's an editor at the newspaper in Midland. Her husband went to Afghanistan, and once when I was visiting, the power went out and he was pre-

pared for war again. Their home is brick and their daughter is blonde. They drive a hybrid.

"You don't have to feel bad about wanting to stay at home with your kids."

"It's just—"

It's because of Megan that I'm a feminist. It's because of her that I'm a writer. When I was eighteen, I wanted so badly to be like her.

"Meg," I said, "listen, it doesn't make you any less of a feminist for wanting to raise your kids. I mean, I'd argue that it kind of makes you more of one, you know?"

"Do you really think so?"

I assured her that—shhh, shhh—she was not betraying feminism.

ooooo

Whereas I used to rely on her for advice.

ooooo

Adult friendships are scaffolded with negativity, complaint, empathetic bitching.

ooooo

In our dorm room together that first night, Megan said we were soul mates.

ooooo

A friend is a place; friendship a space.
    The scale is distance, in kilometers and honesty.

ooooo

How souls split up sometimes and never become whole again.

ooooo

And relationships end.

∞∞∞

I keep forcing myself to imagine Johnny Martinez in a hospital room dying and end up remembering how I threaded folios into books while watching my sister die. I pulled the cloth taut to make the covers and gave one to the doctor after he called the time of death.

Then, I asked if he could write me a prescription for Xanax.

∞∞∞

Right now, I actually want to feel sadness.

∞∞∞

Megan texted, "Hey can you talk?"
I called her back and she cried and I didn't.

∞∞∞

I want to feel more sadness.

∞∞∞

Yesterday I was only thinking in hypotheticals, today—

∞∞∞

The sadness I feel is self-satisfying. It doesn't feel legit, like I am bending the body into an impossible shape and just keeping it there, statuesque.

∞∞∞

I call Megan about the funeral. I'd like to go and so would she, and Midland is kind of on the way to Fort Worth, where his parents are transporting his body to bury. I count the hours of driving on my fingers and decide that I can't afford it.

ooooo

Space refuses to contract.

ooooo

I am selfish because I would drive 800 miles every month to see Harold for a weekend, but I can't do the same for the funeral of an old friend.

ooooo

Friendships saunter off when you turn away.

ooooo

Every time I drive to see Harold, I see the turn off to Midland, but I keep on driving east.

ooooo

Dorothy lives seven miles away from me and some days even that short distance seems impossible to approach.
     I can't imagine an identity without Dorothy.

ooooo

The distribution of friends over a map. Run your fingers over its topography and feel the heat of camaraderie rise up like lava bubbles.

ooooo

The last time I saw Megan she wasn't pregnant. I don't know if she had a boy or a girl.

Every time we talk, Megan says something about how great my life is.

As I flail.

The scaling of friendship, its measurement in weight and miles.

How easily friends flit across open geography.

Imagined geographies like projected lives: Johnny Martinez laughs in a home movie. He waves his arms around like a maniac and makes himself into a joke. Everyone is having a really good time.

The first time I go to a real market, I am thirty and in Vietnam with my mother. The city is charged and caffeinated. No matter the time, the markets are always filled. People congregate. They don't form lines. There is no order. Meat glistens its freshness, and the greens pop with depth.

I have travelled across the ocean precisely to go to these markets. Here, my mother and I will pick out cloth and take it to the tailor who will sew me an *áo dài* for my wedding. There will be no ceremony. I already despise Chris and I don't want to get married, but he pressures me and guilts me and berates me until we do.

When my mother and I find silk we like, the vendor gives us a price.

"Aaaay-a," my mother sounds. "That's double what the man in the stall down there is charging." My mother is a keen negotiator. This is the first stall we have been to today.

"Look at this. It's pure silk. And tough." She pulls on the fabric. The pattern barely distorts with the firm stretch.

We walk away content.

Later, my aunt takes me to go buy wedding rings. My aunt pays fifty percent less than the original price. I see a scarlet jade bracelet. It's dark and emotional, as though it has lived already.

I try my hand at haggling, but my limited Vietnamese and bloated face tell the vendor that I do not belong there. My aunt comes over to watch me fail, but I impress myself, staying firm. The vendor doesn't go half price, but it's pretty close.

It takes soap, lotion, a plastic bag, and popping my thumb out of place to get it on. It fits perfectly.

A year and a half later, I will be back in the States and walking down the street. My marriage is abusive, and I fall down on the sidewalk, shattering the bracelet. My left ankle has dislocated and I have to push it back into place. I am crying. It's the pain.

When I show my husband the broken pieces of jade, he tells me I need to look where I'm going.

4

In my quaint desert town, the farmer's market is a place to be seen. It reminds me of when I was Chris's wife, so I haven't gone in years.

ooooo

Months later, I am in New York for a wedding, and my friend Claire and I go to Chinatown. She goes off to buy her children kitsch and I wander around looking for a jewelry store.

Inside, the storeowner asks if I need help.

"Yes," I say in Vietnamese. "I'm looking for a jade bracelet."

He shows me the way, examining my wrists as we walk.

"These will fit you." He shows me an assortment of cheap jade. The green looks artificial and neon. I wish I had dressed more professionally.

"No," I say. "I want the real stuff."

He smiles warmly. "These are very nice, but I have even nicer ones over here."

Again, he shows me the way. We make small talk, and when he learns I am a professor, he's eager to sell me his more expensive goods.

"I'd prefer a red one," I say. I tell him about my broken bracelet, and his sigh doesn't signal empathy. It's more complex than that, something between disappointment and pity.

"Here, let me show you." He pulls out an assortment of red jade bracelets, none of which hold the same gravitas as the one I got in Vietnam, sentimentality, maybe.

"This one." I point inside the glass case at a tri-colored oval bracelet. Traditional jade bracelets are circular.

"Ahhh, this one is a good one. Look at the white," he says. I look. "It ages as you age."

The store is filled with real and imitation gold. The shine makes me squint.

"But I worry it's too small for you."

Originally two hundred dollars, I talk him down one-twenty and leave with bruised fingers and skin.

Later, when I tell Claire the story, I will say I haggled him down to a hundred flat.

The market is open for negotiation.

oooo

When I visit my parents, my mother and I go to a fancy outdoor mall. It's our tradition to go to Nordstrom Rack for bras. My mother tries to pick ones exactly like mine. "We can be similar," she says. She says, "We can be exactly the same now."

oooo

My dealer says, "What are you and your boo doing this weekend? I never see Harry anymore."

He is always trying to insert himself in our relationship, or, to make new friends.

And: no one calls him Harry.

"Oh, I don't know, probably we'll just sit around the apartment and Harold'll play PES all day."

"You should make him take you to White Linen Night. They close down Heights and there are vendors and everyone wears white linen!"

The first time we met, my dealer wouldn't let me step on his carpet. Now I am careful when I enter. I move from tile to tile, never touching fiber.

oooo

Later that night, Harold will tell me he slept with another woman and I will feel ruined and I will decide to stay three more days with him—and pretend. For the past three years we have been pretending. For the past three years he has said unforgivable things and done unforgivable things and then he's asked me to pretend it didn't happen. "Just stay 'til Monday," he'd say. "Please?" And he'd shine those eyes at me. "Do you really have to go back today?" Or, "You were planning on staying 'til Monday anyway." And I would be convinced—because I didn't want to accept things as complete, finished, over.

We don't make plans to go to White Linen Night. As expected, Harold plays PES but he invites me to play along. It's fun. We're fine. I tell myself we're fine. Then we get on our bicycles and head out for adventure. It's hot in Houston and my pink hair dye runs with sweat. I feel like a feminist poser, talking a big game about empowerment but living a reality of passivity and self-contempt. Otherwise, I would not be able to justify staying.

Outside a record store, the streets have been shut down and vendors begin to set up their tents. Inside, we pass headphones back and forth at the listening station. Although irritable and feeling fully wrecked, I smile brightly. We leave with no new records.

"I'm thirsty," I say.

It must be over a hundred degrees and the humidity feels like a stage curtain. Every time the curtain lifts, I imagine a spotlight shining on Harold fucking this other girl. Before he pulls his cock out and comes on her face, he says her name. He isn't confused. He doesn't think it's me. He knows exactly what he's doing. The curtain is my eyelid, blinking revelation away like how you push tears into your skin before the lights come on after a movie.

We walk our bikes past several vendors. I love watching my pedals rotate as I push the bicycle forward. I leave him at an amateur art stand and go looking for a drink by myself. Later, I come back and he's talking to the artist. He's a photographer. He displays landscapes that look like really big postcards.

"What do you think about this one?" He points to a Photoshopped picture of an oilrig. Harold works in oil and gas. It fits.

"It's nice," I say.

"Yesterday," he says to the artist, "I had paintings on my walls and then she took them all away."

His facts are true. I am portrayed as a thief, but those paintings are mine. I imagine Harold bringing this girl he fucked into his apartment, how she makes some banal compliment about the paintings, how her panties are already at her ankles. Where am I? I'm probably waiting for him to call me.

"How much do you want for it?" I ask. If the price is right, I just might buy it for him.

He says three hundred and I scoff. "How about a hundred?"

"Do you know art?" he asks me. "Do you anything about art?"

The photographs are very large and most of them look like they've gone through an Instagram filter.

"This is a photograph," I say, "not a painting." And, "You can make as many duplicates as you want."

People in white linen begin to buzz and swarm. They pull coolers full of beer, and everyone is drinking from open containers on the open street, even the policemen are holding brown bags, as if White Linen Night were a state of exception and all laws are suspended for the affluent to play for an evening.

"Three hundred is nothing. Go to any gallery!"

"This isn't a gallery," I say.

It isn't nighttime yet. This place will become mayhem.

"I don't want your money." He tries to pretend I am not making him cry. He says, "Both of you can just leave."

"Hey now," I say, "I'm sorry. This isn't my purchase. Why don't you two talk more and I'll go. I've offended you and I'm sorry." I wasn't sorry, but I felt empathetic humiliation for him.

His face is red, but I can't tell if it's the sun or emotions. "You don't even know. I've spent thousands of dollars travelling all over the world to take these pictures, and now you're insulting my art?"

I leave. A few stalls down I negotiate three miniature paintings of chickens from thirty to twenty dollars. I don't buy them and feel victorious.

∞∞∞

I am an academic, and I am on the market this year. The market strangles self-confidence. It ushers in demoralization so deep you feel like a fly hopeless in molasses. The job market is the destination for hundreds of over-qualified applicants all vying for a handful of jobs.

One year, at MLA, I saw a man in a fit of hysteria. There was fresh Chicago snow melting on his coat and head. It looked like he'd spent hours styling his hair and everything was ruined. His suit was bought off a rack. It hadn't been tailored and the shoulders were too broad, the hips too tight. He screamed at the concierge, "What do you mean there's no coat check?"

She replied, "I'm sorry, sir, but we just don't have one. You could leave it at the front desk if you'd—"

"Do you know what's going on here? This is the most important interview of my life and I'm wearing a blue coat with a black suit—" His voice quieted to a defeated whisper. "—and who is ever going to hire me now?"

Outside the conference hotel are huddles of smokers looking like a funeral but more stressed.

ooooo

Harold and I go to the flea market. It's an adventure because he exists above the flea market, whereas I used to go every weekend with my mother when I was still young.

He buys a lenticular puzzle for us to do together, and I end up putting it together by myself.

ooooo

"Okra is good for bowel movements," my mother says. "How are your bowel movements?"

"Good," I say and blush. "They're fine."

My mother's cancer is in remission, but her colon doesn't relent.

I can understand why she's asking, but that doesn't lessen the humiliation.

"We have to go to the market later," my mother says, and I think she means supermarket. "They have the best okra. It's—" and my mother switches to English, "organic."

My mother directs as I drive. She points to every passing car, tells me to be careful. My eyes follow my mother's finger there and then there and I swerve. My mother points again, "Be careful."

On a dirt lot next to the bank, farmers have set up tents. It's hot in San Antonio, even though it's still early. The humidity pulls the air down and thickens it.

"Be sure to haggle," my mother says.

I save a whole dollar because I buy two pints of okra instead of one.

Later, I will cook the okra for Harold. He will help himself to another serving.

The next day, I will find a receipt for condoms from Amazon in his apartment. I will practice my lines. When he gets home, I will say, "So are you cheating on me or do you plan on it?"

"Neither," he will say.

At that moment, he doesn't have his dick in anyone else; ostensibly, he will not be lying.

It will be a few more days yet before he admits he was cheating. Even though I know, I will be surprised—even though I knew it all along.

ooooo

"Pretend," I remind myself, "and it will all be OK."

ooooo

Hundreds of drunk people in white linen cloud around me. White people wearing white linen. I am wearing a floral shirt and blue shorts. Harold is wearing neon. He pulls a pale blue button-up from his bike bag. "Does this look any better?" he asks.

White privilege means walking into any room and feeling immediately accepted.

"Let's go," Harold says. "I feel stupid."

This must be the first time he has felt alienated.

Whereas I have the wrong skin and the wrong salary.

Weeks later, when I am back in the desert and my tenure file is about to be due and I am on an intense book deadline and the semester is already a monster, he will say something about how his next girlfriend will be—at the very least—presentable. I will hang up the phone while he is still talking, and he will not call back.

ooooo

I buy earrings from a stall at the market. They are made with dangling bullet casings. I pull off the bullets because I think they're tacky.

When the owners of the stall see me at the café, they offer to repair it for free.

∞∞∞

There is no differentiation between prescribed medication and black market drugs in Vietnamese.

∞∞∞

The process of being on the job market bifurcates emotions. First, hope. A powerful optimism that this year will be the year, finally, finally, yes yes yes. Next, contempt. For the place you live and the place you work. You must tell yourself you hate your life. You must hate every aspect of your life. You must be miserable. This is the only way you can convince yourself to go through the trauma of the market.

Hundreds pared down to ten.

At MLA, you sit on a bed to interview. You hope your suit doesn't shift too much while you speak. You try not to gesticulate too much. You try to keep your words sharp. You fake it all.

You wait by the phone, just the same as I wait by the phone. You hold it in your fists, hoping it will vibrate, make some kind of sound, but it remains silent and still.

If the phone rings, which mine hasn't, you will be invited to a campus visit, and it is two days of examination by microscope. You are bacteria.

Hundreds pared down to ten, pared down to three.

You wait by the phone. You hold it in your palm, hoping it will vibrate, make some kind of sound, but it remains silent and still.

And you get not a phone call but an email. You were a finalist for the job. Maybe the chair of the search committee will be cruel and tell you that you were second choice but oh so close. Sorry, this is just the market.

∞∞∞

Stalls of stinky fish in Chinatown and the sidewalk is always wet, like puddles of dog urine on my parents' floor.

ooooo

A good wife goes to the market and buys berries, which she will bake into a pie. The crust is made with cold butter. This used to be me.

ooooo

In the US, there are more than 300 MFA program, more than 30 PhD in Creative Writing. Conservatively saying five per genre graduating per year, you do the math. This year, 41 tenure track openings in fiction, 15 for poetry, 19 for creative non-fiction.

It is the thrill of victory against impossible odds. This is what you wager for. And you lose. You are a loser.

ooooo

Crossing into Cambodia, I see large rafts along the ocean shore. I ask my aunt what they are. She tells me that this is where you go to get the freshest fish. She says, "But you have to be careful which side you buy from. Never buy from Cambodians. They put their children on the streets to beg for money."

ooooo

"I've never been here before," my first boyfriend told me on our first date. "This place is kind of a meat market."

ooooo

When I leave my parents' house, my car is filled with groceries from the Vietnamese market.

ooooo

I interviewed for my first Women's Studies class in the café in the farmer's market in South Bend, IN.

I tell my psychiatrist, "I'll just buy it off the street," and he prints out the prescription.

I am keenly aware of the social class of the men I date, their earnings and potential.

Harold talks to me about his stocks and asks if I am impressed. He asks me how much capital I have, how much student debt, and I think this is a sign that we are becoming more serious, but he just wants to know that he's better than me.

Dorothy and I walk through Market Square in San Antonio. She buys two Mexican dresses and I buy a Ronaldo jersey for Harold.

Later, he will say, "Ronaldo? I can't wear a Ronaldo jersey. People will think I'm a Ronaldo fan."

Later, he will say, "Why didn't you get me Robben jersey?"

"They only had two options. I've told you that," I will say. "Ronaldo and Messi. I figured you'd want Ronaldo more."

He will put it on and ask if he looks fat.

But before I am made to feel like a disappointment, Dorothy and I are laughing and it feels so good to be with my friend. We order aguas frescas from the fruteria and listen to the sounds of the market. We are no longer writers and professors. We are the anonymous dollars we can spend, and so we do.

A.

When Harold and I break up, I set reminders on my phone for every thirty minutes to instruct me not to call him. My index finger hovers over that green icon, like breath waiting to intersect with skin.

B.

It is snowing and the Little Match Girl stands outside. She strikes a wooden match and lets the fire prick at her fingers.

She looks through a window of a house and inside there is a family laughing and being together.

Her nails are very dirty. She would never go in, even if they invited her.

She drops a hot match, and it makes a single black dot against all that fluorescent snow.

C.

My sister was dying, and I needed any asshole at all to buy me dinner. For those few hours, I could be anyone: I imagined telling him I'm a primate anthropologist or a nurse. And my sister could not be dying. I didn't meet Harold that night, but a week later, he texted me, "So you don't drink?"

"No. I'm allergic," I texted back.

"That sucks."

I was sitting in the ICU. My sister was hooked up to all sorts of machines. Once, I took a picture for my father, who was too weak to visit, but she looked so scary—so un-beautiful—that I couldn't show him. I was folding paper into books, gluing cloth to dense boards: I was sewing. Outside, a storm was only threatening.

"So, want to watch me drink a beer?"

My sister died later that night. Harold invited me over and I spent the next month in a chaste bed with him, making adventures and playing board games. Nearly three years and many heartbreaks later, he still charms me.

∞∞∞

Opportunity rolled past me on his golden ball and I yanked that tuft of hair so hard: when I fall asleep on Harold's chest, he strokes my hair, which is still wet from our shower. He doesn't want his sheets smelling like smoke.

∞∞∞

Three years later, out of revenge and injury and desire, I meet a man from fifteen years ago, and I know, immediately, that he is my Metanoia, but I cannot look in that mirror. I cannot see who I have become.

∞∞∞

When I was married to Chris and we argued, he would call me a selfish bitch.

I worry that I am.

∞∞∞

Harold is shopping for groceries and I am sitting in my sunroom critiquing student stories. He calls me and says, "Have you had sex with anyone?"

"Why?"

"So you have."

"I didn't say that."

"But you have, I know you have."

Later that night, I text and ask if he's going to break up with me now.

He texts back, "I could feel it. Like I knew exactly when it happened."

He tells me he's never felt anything like that before. He almost threw up. His stomach plummeted down somewhere. He couldn't breathe. This, he tells me, is exactly how I feel, too, about him—except all the time. I name this anxiety, I name it love.

D.

After he's been picked up at the Circle K across the street, Justin calls me collect. He says, "I'm sorry, Lily, but I got kidney stones again and they hurt so bad—I didn't know what else to do, well, shit, you're gonna see it anyway. I shot up, OK? I'm man enough to admit that I was weak just that once, but I had to. You don't understand. It just hurt so bad."

It's not like I didn't know: his erratic behavior, disappearing into his room for a week at a time, those evil eyes. He had me convinced that he hid in his room whenever he ran out of Xanax because his anxiety was so severe. I believed him because I needed to, because I couldn't handle my own life. I couldn't shoulder his life, too.

"So don't freak out when you see the needles, OK?"

Justin will be extradited back to Texas for violating his probation by living with me. Well, technically, for fleeing the State of Texas. And his piss test will be dirty. He's already been through Rehab for Felons. He's been in a halfway house. I'm scared and angry—at everybody. Not wanting to chase ghosts, I pay a friend to clean out Justin's room. He finds a lot of needles. "Yeah," my friend says, "there's no way he just started shooting up while you were out of town."

I need to balance disappointment with boundaries: he has no one else and I can't let him back in my house.

E.

Halfway to her grandmother's house, the girl looks left to the path of sharp pins with primary color baubles. Then she looks right to the path of needles with its many squinting eyes. She rejects feminine domesticity entirely, turns right around in her little red ballet flats and goes back to work.

According to Ovid, it is Dionysus who grants him the golden touch. The hunger inside him like an arch, swaying over empty air. After twenty-four hours, his body's glycogen stores are depleted. His insulin is low and his glucagon is too high. Energy is produced through lipolysis. Glucopeogenesis turns glycerol into glucose and more biochemical stuff happens and happens until he dies, literally, of starvation. Golden fungus grows under his esophagus. The blind radiant statues surrounding him witness nothing.

∞∞∞

When I show up to work with a black eye during finals week, I tell everyone that I dropped a plate on my face when I was on my tippy-toes reaching for it on a shelf just out of my reach. "I was too lazy to get a step ladder," I say cutely. "I'm short." I shrug at my non-joke, and we fake laugh uncomfortably at my obvious lie.

A month later, Chris disappears from the desert like Houdini and I don't talk about it with anyone at work. Even though he used to adjunct there, my colleagues never ask about him. It's like he was never here and I was never married and all of my suffering gets filed under "Do Not Discuss," right after "Abortion" and before "Genocide."

With my friends, I celebrate. I begin eating meat again and it's no wonder to me that I denied myself such satisfaction for nearly half of my life, my masochist personality.

∞∞∞

Yesterday, on the phone, my father said, "You're of the age that you need to exercise. At least one hour a day. You're too fat."

Last week, on the phone, my father said, "You look better in button-up shirts because it hides your fat belly."

Two weeks ago, on the phone, my father said, "You need to wear high heels. It will make you look less dumpy." My father said, "At least two inches."

On my last day visiting last month, my father said, "Have you gained kilos?"

And my mother said, "Leave her alone." We are both surprised at my father's restraint, that he had been able to hold back his criticism for so long.

∞∞∞∞

When I first got to the desert, my colleagues used to invite me out to do things. Chris came along, of course, and over the course of the evening he kept score. Afterwards he would scream at me, listing out all the men I had flirted with and all the women I had flirted with and he'd scream, "How dare you disrespect our relationship like that?"

And he'd scream, "How dare you emasculate me?"

And more quietly, "In public."

After a few hours, I'd confess my sins and worry about how noise travels through such dry and hot air.

My colleagues in the department don't know any of this, but they no longer invite me out. I try to figure out what I've done wrong to deserve this ostracization, this out-casting. I'm too weird, I decide, and they are too square.

Even among academics, I don't belong.

∞∞∞∞

It used to be my father would give me the first cut of barbeque. Then I became a vegetarian, which he hated. Then I stopped being a vegetarian, which made him happy, but he still eats the first cut himself.

∞∞∞∞

"Open," Harold says, and he feeds me steak straight off the grill.

Later, he says, "Close your peepers," and he places his fingertips on my eyelids. His touch is gentle and I fall asleep because he has commanded it.

∞∞∞∞

Imagine his fingers. The pale rind, once oxygenated, clings to his nails and skin. His fingers are tarred a deep humid brown. Hades licks them, as if to clean, but his tongue only lifts away the tart reports of broken fruit.

He is in love: his desperation is urgent and obvious. She has taken all his power and refused to eat. His crown and cock ring are locked in a drawer. Nothing belongs to him anymore.

But he isn't really a man at all. Nor is a king. He is a god, and the Underworld is his domain.

Imagine Persephone, her elusive body, so fragile now it may rip apart. But she must stay resolute. She cannot eat, must not, because even Persephone knows what the Fates decreed: any being that consumes in the Underworld must stay there, forever.

Persephone misses the sun, grass under her toes, wind. It's been weeks since she's eaten and all that remains is a slow acidic ache, nothing urgent, just her body breaking down from malnutrition.

Every day she denies herself food she becomes more beautiful.

She is a temptress now, an anorexic vixen.

She is the wife of a god, too, but only because he won't let her go home.

Imagine Persephone before: a shadow-haired beauty, maybe a procession of fauna pursuing her, flowers and ferns extending their petals towards her heat. She is the origin of the fairy tale princess.

But now: blood so thin it imitates cyanide, morphine, cancer, electricity. It's not just that she dislikes Hades. No, her entire constitution has mutated to rage against him. Efficiency through evolution.

Every day, Hades begs her, "You have to eat. My darling, please," and every day she refuses.

It is in this simple act of refusal that Persephone wields her power. She is a prisoner of war, enduring torture and keeping her secrets close. She sits on a velveteen throne, but it feels as though it is covered in thorns. Her husband scurries into the kitchen, washes vegetables and peels fruit, mixes flour into dough. He garnishes every dish, arranges the silver serving tray just so, offers it to her with his head bowed low.

He's just so—*human.*

She is disgusted.

She walks away, quickly, because she is very, very hungry.

ooooo

She input her name as "Elizabeth Temptress" in Harold's phone.

"Oh that's just Liz." He says, "She wants to be a writer, just like you."

ooooo

Chris was a proselytizing vegetarian. Before we met, he was a proselytizing vegan. I used to make us quinoa and steamed kale every night. Salt was an indulgence. Now that I am no longer married to Chris, I eat fast food and order large slabs of meat.

When we first met, he told me, "I have a borderline eating disorder." He thought he was being vulnerable, as did I, and so I fell in love with him and now we are divorced and I realize the whole scene wasn't vulnerable after all. He was just stating a fact.

Later, when Dorothy and I joke about Chris having Borderline Personality Disorder, neither of us will be joking.

ooooo

I used to have a stash of candy hidden in a purse at the back of the closet. Now, I can have as much as I want.

ooooo

Harold says he cheated on me because Elizabeth Temptress was ruthless in her pursuit. "She wouldn't leave me alone," he scoffs and rolls his eyes and says, "but she's not girlfriend quality," and it's an empty title to him anyway.

ooooo

When I was in second grade, I used to make myself throw up every day after lunch to avoid going to Social Studies. I would almost choke myself coughing so hard. It wasn't that I had body image issues, that would come later and stay forever. It was the shame that I was not good at Social Studies. It was the possibility of disappointing my father if I didn't get straight A+'s. To my father, an A was failure to be perfect.

Once, in Social Studies, I had an assignment to build a neighborhood and my father stayed up all night painting trees and propping them with toothpicks to give dimension. In the morning, he asked me, "Do you think it's beautiful?"

They called my parents in and said I had a disease. They asked if I was hungry, if I felt bad about myself, they tried to get to the bottom of my sickness.

∞∞∞

It's not like I don't know Harold is a liar.

I choose to not know everything I do.

I choose my enforced ignorance.

I choose to be dumb—I choose Harold, every time.

∞∞∞

My father has always loved beautiful things. He likes to make them and photograph them. He is a creator, an inventor. Decades ago he had a stroke and lost sensation in half of his body. Now, the surface of his body is numb, but underneath there is an ache that makes his body convulse as though under threat of fire. This is one of the many pains my father doesn't tell me about, but it's constant.

Instead, I admire his old paintings, the ones he painted right after he retired but before the stroke. I admire his new sketches, which are shaky but elegant. His eye for architecture and the building of things remains constant and careful, like a pruned bonsai garden. "Do you like this one?" He points at a clay pot that he has broken in half. It cradles a simple bonsai tree and a little stone temple. "It still needs a lot of work," my father says, "but I will work hard to finish it before you leave. Maybe you can give it to your boss. Does he like Oriental things?" I say I don't know. When I leave, my father is not yet done with his construction. "It's missing a path," he says. My father was always slow. We used to joke that he was born in the year of the turtle. Now, my father requires even more patience. Everything takes energy and he has almost no control over his body any more. Everything he says is undercut with criticism and defeat. He doesn't have a single friend left. He has alienated and insulted them all away. "I'll have it ready for you next time," he says. When he smiles, I count the missing teeth in his mouth.

∞∞∞

Harold's mother tells him he has scales over his eyes.

I wonder if he blindfolded Elizabeth Temptress before fucking her.

∞∞∞

"I've got a new suitor," I tell my friend Thomas. We are at a bar playing pool and I am drinking a vanilla milk shake. Chris has been gone for years now and Harold and I are taking a break, again.

"I hate it when you say that."

"What?"

"Suitor," he says. He sneers. "You're not a princess, OK?"

"No, but I live in a fairy tale."

He tells me to shut up and we continue to swat at each other's clever digs.

∞∞∞

It is not porridge but foie gras. It is the smell that lures her in, not innocence or travail. Tiramisu makes striated shelves in the refrigerator and duck soufflé rises in the over. Persephone sits on a gilded throne and eats until stuffed. Her hair is yellow, but it looks like silver in cottages at night. She wipes her mouth with the edges of her grimy scarlet ragdoll dress.

∞∞∞

For months I have been texting with a guy from undergrad. I had a devastating crush on Jacob in college and he had rejected me. Now we are adults and I am in love with Harold. My love for him feels desperate sometimes. Other times, it is fulfilling.

"My hedonism could beat up your hedonism," Jacob texts me.

Hedonism to me is a rainbow of pharmaceuticals. It is artificial, chemical. And since the day my sister died, every night has been a hedonist pity-party.

A week later, he texts me, "We should have a hedonist weekend." I agree, because this isn't going to happen. These are just flirty texts absent of possibility.

A week later I am back in Houston with Harold and Jacob texts, "Still up for a hedonist weekend?"

The hypothetical becomes practical.

"What would you like to do?"

"Idk, fun is the only requirement."

"Swingers club it is then." He clarifies, "I was trying to turn to the most hedonistic thing I could think of. Just seeing if we are going to get naked or just get fucked up."

"I wouldn't go to a swinger's club, fyi."

"Neither would I."

I feel guilty, but I don't tell Harold about any of this.

Two days later, he will tell me he cheated on me. I will try to forgive him because in my head I was already fantasizing about fucking this college crush in an anonymous hotel room.

When I was married to Chris, he'd taught me that thinking was the same as doing. Thinking alone was proof of guilt. Like the time he accused me of having a threesome with a visiting writer and my best friend's husband during a reception we were hosting. He said my introduction had been too effusive. With students and colleagues still in my house, he said, "Everyone noticed," and everyone directed their attention at us. "You made a mockery of our relationship in front of everyone. I hope you feel embarrassed. How dare you disrespect me like that? Emasculate me? You're such a selfish bitch." And he kept on going and the party shuffled out whatever door was closest, I shut down for hours. Not once had I ever even considered a threesome but by the end of his shouting, I admitted that yes, I was a selfish bitch who emasculated him in public because I disrespected our relationship.

I'd done nothing though. I've done nothing.

I'm not a cheater.

I try and fail to forgive him.

ooooo

About half of his body, my father says, "I can't feel a thing." He puffs on his pipe and smiles at me. His teeth are rotting and he needs to go back to Vietnam to get them extracted but he's not strong enough to travel. My father says, "But it always aches."

Over the phone my mother says, "He can't even chew. We had to eat porridge last night." I clench my jaw and my teeth electrify. Back when I was married, I used to grind my teeth in my sleep. Now I don't sleep and my jaw is still sore in morning.

ooooo

When my friends ask how I can possibly still love Harold, I say, "We have fun together."

I say, "It's the first time I've had fun in my life."

I say, "Harold taught me fun."

And I am afraid that without him, I will lose that experience—and him, I would lose him.

ooooo

My sexual desires have changed now that I am in my thirties. Before, Chris used to beg for sex and I would give it to him in order to avoid an argument that would lead to him shouting at me for hours and me shutting down.

After not seeing each other all month, when I drive 800 miles to Houston, I still beg Harold to fuck me and some days he would say he just wasn't feeling it. Things make sense, much later.

I masturbate every day.

ooooo

Dionysus loves to fuck against vines of honeysuckle.

∞∞∞

"Fairly rough sex. Light bondage stuff. You?"

∞∞∞

Harold watches porn as he fucks me. Maybe he looks at me, too, but my eyes are always closed.

∞∞∞

Rather than end things, I ask Harold for a break until he visits me in a few weeks for Labor Day. I text him, "I can't go worrying about where you stick your dick between now and then."

A break is nothing new. For the past three years our relationship has taken every form. We have been polyamorous. We have broken up. We have been fuck buddies. We have been lovers. We have been monogamous. Or, I had been monogamous at least. I tell him he can go do whatever he wants until Labor Day. And in his freedom lives mine.

Ten days later, I will knock on a wooden door at Hotel Andaluz in Albuquerque. Jacob will open the door, kiss me then push me hard against the wall, and I will notice how fragile his wrists are. "Am I being too rough?" he will ask.

"No," I will say, "this is exactly how I want it."

∞∞∞

Once, when we were broken up, Harold told me he would cheat on his wife with me. "I'll always want you," he said. We were sitting in the bathtub and it was his birthday and I told him his future will be lonely and miserable.

∞∞∞

The old crone's house is made of large slabs of cookies spiced with turmeric and ginger. Laces of saffron contrast the raw umber. Columns of roasted pig support the house and the roof is shingled with gnocchi. Cream sauce drips like icicles in the early spring.

It has been days since our father abandoned us, and we are starving.

"Should we knock first?" Persephone asks me. She doesn't wait for me to answer.

Our father should have taught us better manners.

∞∞∞

Harold chose a pale version of me: a wannabe poet—and white.

Later, I wonder how much paltry poetry she has written about him and posted on Facebook in its entirety.

Months later, she goes to a friend's book launch. He tells me she showed up drunk, went up to him and said they have a friend in common, said she stole my boyfriend. She insisted on taking a picture together so she could post it on social media so I could see them together and smiling. My friend looks very uncomfortable, and Elizabeth Temptress radiates victory.

∞∞∞

"You should eat in proportion to your size," Chris told me, back when he was still my husband. He showed me his bowl and compared it to mine "You are two-thirds my size so you should eat one-third less than me."

I felt ashamed and tried to eat less and exercise more.

∞∞∞

What pisses me off more: that he chose her or that he couldn't find someone better than me or that I wasn't enough.

∞∞∞

The hotel is decadent. Slats of stained glass dangle from the tall ceilings. The doors are made of heavy oak. The suite is large and hip, and he has thrown the drapes on the ground. "Faux leather," he says, "offends my aesthetics." The sheets have a high thread count. The pillows are down. He says, "Get on the bed now," and I follow his instructions because I have always been a perfect student.

ᴏᴏᴏᴏᴏ

Two years after Chris left, I made coffee the way I did every morning. Still sleepy and wandering around the kitchen, I found a pomegranate. I hadn't bought the fruit since he left. My memory of him was knotted with resentment and anger. I refused to buy pomegranates because they were his favorite, but I'd had a party the night before and one of my friends must have brought it. I turned on the light and it revealed the disarray of my kitchen. Knives crusted with goat cheese and butter cream cake.

As I separated the fruit from its rind, my fingers removing one seed at a time, I felt sudden affection: I remembered the way his impatience with my process made his smile boyish, innocent, as if it touched him, how he scooped fistfuls at a time. Those nights we watched television, and together, we hid from the monster our relationship had become. Our sticky fingers would interlace and all of our turbulence and turmoil would calm into tender sleep.

ᴏᴏᴏᴏᴏ

Jacob makes me come twice. He pulls my hair back to kiss me. He says, "Do you want my cock?" He says, "Tell me you want it." I tell him and he fucks me seven more times that night. I open my mouth when he tells me he's about to come.

ᴏᴏᴏᴏᴏ

I haven't forgotten about my dead sister.

My parents' bodies put them in a constant state of dysphoria. I go in search of euphoria.

To impress Jacob, I tell him about my interest in rats and psychological experiments. His skin is soft and very pale. He is as handsome as he was at eighteen. The hair above his ears has begun to gray and he looks fashionably distinguished.

He asks if I've heard of the study where rats were administered small doses of heroin when they pushed a lever and they'd push it until they died. I kiss him because I hadn't heard of the experiment and because his intelligence attacks my body like a virus filled with desire.

I have tangled the fairy tales I write with my life.

He was terribly hungry for me.

I don't tell Jacob about the potions in my bag. It is the first night I go to sleep without a sleeping pill and anxiety medication since my sister died and I sleep a full eight hours for the first time in months.

The next morning we joke about the night before and I worry that I've offended him by falling asleep twice while he was talking to me. I text Dorothy about this and she says, "Well you were tired." And then she adds, "You were tired because you were getting your brains fucked out of you."

She does not yearn for his kiss because she is sleeping. In her sleep, the pain of wicked spells and an eternity of dormancy makes her dream of a very handsome Charming to release her. When he parts her lips, her mouth smells of rot.

∞∞∞

Before I found her seizing on the floor of her bedroom, before she died, I watched my sister polish off a ninety-count bottle of Hydros. She gave her son Justin some, but the rest she ate as if garnished with the finest sea salt. She doesn't die of overdose, but she dies.

My doctor ups my dosage of Xanax. There are too many things I can't think about.

∞∞∞

Dionysus is the god of epiphany, the god who comes.

∞∞∞

The only time Harold kissed me the way Jacob does was after rough anal sex. "I feel like I just raped you," he said afterwards.

∞∞∞

Years ago, before my sister died, my mother called me and said, "She hurts so much. It's too much hurt for one person." She was talking about my sister and her brain aneurysm, which was along her spinal cord and caused severe pain. "Just last night," my mother said, "she fell asleep at dinner because of all her medicine."

My sister was prescribed Oxy and Methadone, for the pain.

"I think the medicine is too strong," my mother said.

"I think she's taking too much medicine."

My mother agreed with me, but we were talking about two completely different things.

∞∞∞

Already, the moon had crested: it was late into the night.

A servant announced, "My Queen, this old crone," he rotated his body to point the crown of his head towards the old crone, "claims to be a princess and would like to seek refuge and a warm bed here tonight."

The old crone had a hunched back and unsightly moles all over her face and hands. She was wearing a combination of rags and animal pelts.

Her hair, however, was halcyon and her eyes were flashes of nectary hyacinth.

And so it was that the old crone ascended the wooden ladder. It was a slow process and her joints creaked loudly. Up and up she went. Up past twenty mattresses made of the finest goose down and twenty mattresses of the most miniature pony hair and when she finally made it to the top she let her body fall into the softness.

She was exhausted.

When sunlight shone through the stained glass windows, the old crone hobbled her way down to the queen and her son. She said, "Thank you for your generosity, Charming, but I must ask you one more favor."

Charming's face screwed into something like contempt. "Anything," he said with a courtesy indicative of fine breeding.

"May I please, with your permission and your mother's, be granted one more night in your palace? You see, the bed you offered me was perhaps too hedonic, for I slept not five minutes last night. It felt as though there were a steel rod upright against my spine. Never I have felt such discomfort, so please, dear Prince Charming, may I stay just one more night and perhaps sleep on a more modest bed? I fear my comfort requires simplicity over indulgence."

Now Charming was well-versed in stories of magic and royalty. He knew the old crone would instantly transform into a beautiful princess: perhaps with their first kiss, or marriage, or its consummation. But all those things happened and the old crone remained an old crone and it was only long after the young prince had become a manly king and then an old wise king and then a dead king that the old crone revealed herself not as a princess at all but a queen, old and stately.

ooooo

Electrodes are placed on a rat's hedonic brain. When it pushes the lever, the rat receives a small electrical pulse, which releases pleasure.

Some rats push the lever up to seven hundred times per hour. "This area of the brain is called the pleasure center," Jacob says. My head is on his chest, and sweat condenses in the small spaces between our bodies.

The next morning, he will tell me the secret to a happy marriage is a king-sized bed and two sinks. "It's like men and women run at two different temperatures. I had this girlfriend once who slept under like seven duvets, but at night she'd get hot and throw them all on me. In the morning, she'd get all pissed that they covers were on the ground."

"She was the one who yelled at you all the time?"

"Yeah, she was so unreasonable. Like I was supposed to sleep under fifteen layers of down or something."

We are snuggled close on a king-sized bed. There are two sinks in the bathroom.

∞∞∞

When I visit, from the kitchen, my mother croons, "Aiiiii-ya," and continues cooking. Now that she is retired, she makes elaborate meals for my father, which he criticizes but he always finishes his bowl and serves himself seconds.

∞∞∞

According to the marriage formula, one negative comment has equal value to five compliments. No partner has ever praised me five times in a day, not the man I married, not the man who just broke me, the one I can't release. Once, he'd said, "I don't want you to go getting a big head or anything." Once, he'd said, "Did it hurt your feelings that I didn't say you're beautiful?"

∞∞∞

When Harold says he loves me, I believe him.

Still, I can't respond.

The weight of my love measured against the weight of my life without him measured against his betrayal and all the terrible things he's told me over the years. In the end, no matter my options, I know I will choose Harold.

Over dinner, Jacob says, "You've done pretty well for yourself." It seems absurd that he would think this. My self-esteem has many vacant rooms for rent. It's not that I don't believe him, it's that his praise makes me feel confident and that feels uncomfortable, unnatural, maniacal.

He compliments me many more times as the evening cools us with its mountain air, but it's New Mexico in August and heat pervades everything, even the sublime scenery.

When the wolf tells me to throw my dress into the fire, I do, but not without protest.

When the wolf tells me to throw my britches into the fire, I do, but not without protest.

What I didn't protest at all, however, was the delicious soup he'd made me, with wine-soaked teeth and chewy ear rinds. That I ate with earnestness, as though I had not been fed all week. A girl must mind her manners in the company of strange men and animals.

When the wolf tells me to get into bed, I do, but not without protest. He says, "You didn't tell me you liked to be choked."

I tell him, "I didn't need to."

Even though Harold told me he cheated on me, I stayed in Houston for three more nights. I nested my head on his chest and anchored my body over his. This is how we fall asleep every night except the nights when he breaks up with me.

Two days after my return to the desert, I texted him and said I just couldn't do it. He said he was sorry and he was going to block me. He texted, "So that this is over."

I blocked him, too.

This had never happened before. We were actually breaking up. It felt like the implosion of a star into a black hole. It seemed at once predictable and impossible. I needed it to be impossible.

I held my phone in my hand. It was heavy with mourning. I wished and prayed for it not to be over, for me to able to forgive him, for him to still want me.

The next morning, he emailed and I rejoiced.

But before that next morning ever happens, before I break up with him, I'm over at my friend Scott's place and he goes, "That dude fucked you up." He makes a caveman grunting sound that fits his personality splendidly. "You're so seriously fucked up now."

ooooo

It was the village's hedonism, after all, that caused the infestation. Goose fat and beer bellies for one and all, even the little vagrant children were gluts and their trashcans were a delight for the rats.

I strolled in and played a colorful tune and the rats followed me through the village and across the meadow and into the woods and through the pure white sand and far into the ocean.

Later, the villagers called me a witch and threw me back into the ocean.

Because witches can swim, I lured the children into the salt water. The deeper you go, the lonelier it gets, and so we clasp our hands tightly together and saline deposits glitter along our skin.

ooooo

Harold thinks I've maxed out with him, that I can do no better.

ooooo

"But this psychologist in Vancouver or Toronto or somewhere in Canada—" Jacob shrugs. He is lacing up his Converse. I am sitting on the couch of our hotel suite. The bed is a mess and he is packed. "—whatever, it doesn't matter. So this Canadian psychologist thought, what if we didn't put the rats in steel cages and under harsh conditions? What if we made them comfortable? You have to understand that the other study I told you about was like a breakthrough in addiction research. That's important." When he finishes this story, he will kiss me and then he will leave and there's a chance I will never see him again. "So this Canadian guy built this huge rat haven full of everything a rat loves: a wheel, nests, places for them to play, and rather than look at them in isolation, he puts a whole group of rats in there, like thirty males and thirty females."

He is a forensic neuropsychologist: he is an adult. I find everything about him impressive.

"So like the other study, he introduces them to heroin using the lever system, and guess what happens."

His eyes, like Harold's, are green, but they are two very different men.

"What," I say.

"A small segment of the population, like the same as in humans with addiction, get hooked on heroin, but the majority of the rats just use it periodically, if at all."

"Wow," I say, and I'm genuinely amazed.

I reach for my notebook because I have a terrible memory. I write down, "Rats happiness heroin addiction."

∞∞∞

Despite the sword and ball of golden thread, theirs is not a marital bliss. One night, Theseus turns on the bedroom light and it's late, maybe three in the morning, and says, "You lying bitch, you told me Dorothy texted you first but you texted her first," and he pelted the phone at Ariadne's face. This is where our stories differ: I kept my husband for another couple months and Ariadne dumped hers immediately.

If Chris was my Theseus, Harold is my Dionysius, my god of excess and turmoil. Some say Dionysius rode in valiantly after Theseus abandoned her and saved her from sorrow. Others claim they were married long before the Minotaur was even put in the maze, that she had run away with Theseus in blind lust. Others still argue that the two were never romantically attached, that they were never in love and that this love was never pure. But they would be wrong. The hurt Harold exacted on me is lasting, and all the minotaurs have gone extinct.

Or maybe Harold isn't my Dionysius at all. Maybe not every love story fits neatly into previous love stories. I am looking for the Fates to intervene here, but they, too, have gone extinct. Now there are only humans left to toil without divine interruption, and rats to eat their remains.

ooooo

When I was young, my mother would cuddle me closely when I was sick. She would say, "Shhh, shhh," and tell me that she wanted me to give her all of my sickness, so that she would be sick and I wouldn't. She would suffer for me. I started crying and pulled my sick and contagious body far away from her.

ooooo

It is not a wolf but a prince and his name is Charming. They are not pigs but little girls with delicate snouts and curly pigtails. After going to the market and going to the store, the three little girls eat and they eat, and they want to remain little forever but they can't. They must marry, and Charming knocks on their door. It is not three houses but one, and it is made of stick windows and purple brick. Inside, the furniture is braided straw. It is not a bone slipper but a steel knife, and this is not how the story ends. Out comes the knife and one little girl huffs and another one puffs and the last one pushes Charming right out the door. Together, they celebrate with moscato and warmed brie, sisters and friends and wives to each other.

POST-SCRIPT

As the fairy tale goes, it is the Rat who crosses the threshold of the Great Race first.

And then the Ox.

And then the Tiger.

And then the Rabbit.

And then the Dragon.

And then the Snake.

And then the Horse.

And then the Goat.

And then the Monkey.

And then the Rooster.

And then the Dog.

And then—finally—the Pig.

ACKNOWLEDGMENTS

The author would like to thank the following journals, presses, and anthologies for publishing early versions of these essays: *Alice Blue Review*, Essay Press EP Series, *Festschrift Volume 4: Rikki Ducornet*, *Feminist Wire*, Future Tense's Instant Future eBook Series, *Litscapes: Collected US Writings 2015*, *Pastelogram*, *Scarlet*, *The Spectacle*, *Sonora Review*, *Quarterly West*, and *The Volta*.

In addition to the editors who published very early versions of these essays in their excellent journals and presses, the author would also like to express her gratitude to Rikki Ducornet for their summer fairy tale together and Carmen Giménez Smith for their daily fairy tales together, without whose mentorship this book would have never been possible. She would like to thank the Department of English and the College of Arts and Sciences at New Mexico State University for the grants that afforded her the time and travel to complete this book. Humble thanks to the following friends and readers, thank you, thank you: Kate Bernheimer (not only for providing me with the Light as a Feather exercise but also all her unwavering support over the years), Tom Burnham, Molly Gaudry, Sabrina Gomez, Richard Greenfield, Scott Holcomb, Frances Hwang, Savannah Johnston, Bhanu Kapil, Savannah Johnston, Evan Lavender-Smith, Gene Morgan, Brandon Mundt, Justin Prado, Matthew Salesses, Selah Saterstrom, Anthony Stagliano, Mathias Svalina, Allison Titus, James Underhill, Jackie Wang, Justine Wells, and Joshua Marie Wilkinson. Finally, thank you to Wayne Koestenbaum for believing in the potential of this manuscript and Caryl Pagel for her prudent editorial guidance.

And thank you, mostly, to my parents: *Con chúc bo mẹ phước như Đông Hải, thọ tỉ Nam Sơn.*